Complete Guide to Fasting

A complete guide to fasting, for men and women who want to find out all fasting benefits and improve their lifestyle.

Kaitlyn Terrell

Table of Contents

A complete Guide for Men and Women who want to find out fasting benefits and improve their lifestyle. 10

What is fasting? 11

Best Ways to Do Intermittent Fasting: 13

The 5:2 Diet Plan: 14

    How to do it? 16

Health Benefits Of 5:2 Diet plan: 17

    Weight loss and belly fat reduction: 18

    Other health benefits: 20

Risks Of 5:2 diet plan: 22

What to eat during 5:2 method of intermittent fasting: 25

The 16/8 method: 28

    How to do it? 30

    Recommended foods during 16/8 fasting method: 32

Risks Of 16/8 intermittent fasting method: 36

Benefits of the 16/8 method of intermittent fasting: 38

    Prevention Against diseases: 39

    Extended Life Span: 41

Weight loss: 42

Eat Stop Eat: 44

How to do it?..47

Health Benefits of Eat Stop Eat: 49

Weight loss: 49

Change In body Metabolism: 51

Side Effects of Eat Stop Eat Method: 53

Insufficient Nutrition:....................................54

Low Level of blood sugar:..............................55

Hormonal Changes: 56

Psychology Impact of Eat stop Eat method:............58

The Warrior Method: Fast during Day and Eating at Night:...59

How to do it?..61

Detox (week 1)..61

High fat (week 2) 62

Concluding fat loss (week 3) 63

Health benefits of the warrior Diet: 65

Weight loss: 65

Fights inflammation:.....................................66

Improved Brain Health:..................................67

Risks of the Warrior diet plan:...............................68

What to eat during the warrior diet plan?.................69

Alternate Day Fasting: 72

How to do it?...73

Health benefit of Alternate-day Fasting: 74

Type 2 Diabetes: 74

Weight loss: 76

Heart Health:...76

Autophagy: 78

What to eat During Alternate Day fasting? 79

Risks of alternate-day fasting:.........................81

Some useful tips to fast safely: 83

Drink a lot of water:.................................83

Eat a small amount of food:.........................84

Do not break the fast with huge meals: 84

Go for Walk: 85

Break the fast if not feeling well:....................86

Fasting is not for everyone: 86

Avoid Fasting if:.....................................87

Take Supplements: 88

Eat whole foods when not fasting: 88

Healthy meals to sustain a Healthy Lifestyle:.........90

Fruits and Vegetables:...............................90

Low-fat Milk: 91

Whole Grains, Eggs, and Cereals:....................92

Drink A Lot Of water: 93

Lentils: 93

Fasting and Its Proven Health benefits 94

Control Blood Sugar: 94

Changes Functions of cells and Hormone: 96

Fights Inflammations: 98

Belly Fat Reduction: 99

Improved Heart Health: 101

Boost Brain Cells and Nervous system: 103

Better Growth Hormone Secretion: 104

Long Life Span: 106

Prevents various Kind of Cancers: 107

Helps in better Sleep: 108

Side Effects of Intermittent Fasting: 110

Fatigue: 111

Feeling Hungry Most of the Time: 113

Food Obsessions: 114

Hair Loss: 116

Low Blood sugar: 117

Change in the Menstrual Cycle: 118

Sleep Disturbance: 119

Constipation: 121

Unhealthy meals: 122

Mood Changes: 123

A Healthy Diet Plan for Non-Fasting Hours: 126

Fiber: 127

Calcium: 127

Protein: 128

Carbohydrates: 129

Fats: 130

Myths About intermittent fasting 132

Intermittent fasting leads you towards Starving mode:..133

Skipping breakfast makes you fat: 135

Eating frequency results in better Metabolism: 137

Brain functions better with regular supply glucose: 138

Frequent eating helps in quick weight loss: 140

Frequent eating has many health benefits:........142

Intermittent fasting makes you lose muscles: ...144

Intermittent Fasting provokes the habit of overeating:...145

Your body consumes a certain amount of protein per meal: 147

How to begin intermittent fasting: 148

Identify Goals: 149

Select the Method:...151

Find out caloric needs of the body: 153

Pick up a meal plan:...154

Intermittent fasting for weight loss: All you need to know: 157

You do not have to bind yourself to "8 hours eating window": 159

A shorter Window is more beneficial: 161

Intermittent fasting might not be a long-term weight loss strategy: 162

It is okay to have some cheat days: 163

High Calories Beverages and drinks will break your fast: 164

"Eat Heavy breakfast and light dinner" 165

Intermittent Fasting VS Keto: Should we combine these two? 166

A Right Way to start Intermittent Fasting with Keto Diet: 170

A Menu Guide for Intermittent fasting and Keto: .172

Smoothens Your Path to ketosis: 175

May help you to lose more body fats: 176

Side effects of combining Keto Diet with intermittent fasting: 177

Intermittent fasting for women: 180

Health Benefits of Intermittent Fasting for Women 183

Weight loss: 184

Heart Health: 186

Diabetes: 187

Best Type of intermittent fasting for women: ...189

The fast diet Method: 190

Alternative day fasting: 190

Crescendo Method: 191

Difference between Fasting and Starving: 194

Summary: A Complete Guide to Fasting 201

You must have heard the proverb "Health is wealth". Being healthy means you are up for all the happiness of life. A healthy person is no doubt the wealthiest of all since he can lead his life to the fullest. A healthy lifestyle is the best lifestyle because being healthy does not mean that you have to starve yourself to death or that you have to quit all the foods that you loved at once. It means a healthy and a balanced diet; a diet that is not heavy on your stomach or brain yet has all the important health ingredients including proteins, fibers, fats, vitamins and calcium.

There are a lot of ways that can lead you to a healthy lifestyle. These include walking, cycling, exercising, swimming and fasting. Fasting is one of these healthy activities that need not much but only not eating for some hours. Fasting is the best solution for the people who do not have time to exercise, or have extremely hectic office routines due to which that they cannot find the time to burn some calories. It helps you burn all the stored fats and calories that can be dangerous for your health and can lead to many diseases such as heart attack, diabetes, obesity, laziness and many more.

In this e-book, I am going to address all the questions related to fasting. You might have some questions about fasting, whenever you think about it. The best methods of fasting, how it should be done and its benefits. So, let us have a look at a complete guide to Fasting and its impacts on our health.

A complete Guide for Men and Women who want to find out fasting benefits and improve their lifestyle.

How simple is that, when you fast you are free from all the stress and worries about your calorie intake or how to burn all the calories and a lot of other hassles associated with eating a lot of food. Fasting is a great thing with numerous health benefits but only if it is performed in the right way. So, let's find out what the actual meaning of fasting is and how it should be done.

What is fasting?

The more you fast, the more you learn about fasting and its benefits. There are hundreds and thousands of books that are being written on fasting and how it has a great effect on our health. But until or unless you have tried it, reading those books would not be of any help. Fasting means "Not eating" for a certain period of time. This can be 8 hours, 12 hours or even 14 hours depending on the method that you are using. Fasting has several benefits. It keeps the body active and recycles the blood along with purifying it. Moreover, it helps our body to use the fats that are stored. Fasting is a part of religion as well. People fast differently according to their faiths. You can see religion also cares about human health a lot.

People assume that fasting means starving. It means having no food for long periods. Though that is true, fasting is different from starving. The main purpose of fasting for hours and hours is to make your body healthier and more active and to perform your daily chores in better ways. The fasting practice is becoming very common in different parts of the world. People practice different methods of fasting to reduce body weight and extra fats and to stay more active and younger-looking.

Though there are different kinds and methods of fasting but the one method that is getting popular by the time and most of the people across the world are already following it is known as "intermittent fasting". It is fasting for some irregular hours. Intermittent fasting is different from other kinds of fasting and diet plans because it does not limit the food intake but just the eating hours are limited.

There are different methods of fasting and among them, Intermittent Fasting is the best one.

Best Ways to Do Intermittent Fasting:

Intermittent fasting is one of the best and easiest ways of fasting. Intermittent fasting has a lot of health benefits including weight loss, better metabolic rate and gives a long and healthy life span. There are different ways of intermittent fasting. It depends on the human body and its needs. Different individuals have different tendencies and reactions to intermittent fasting. It is nearly impossible to see the same impact of intermittent fasting on every individual out there, therefore, there are different methods of intermittent fasting for different humans according to their body capabilities and needs.

But the best ones that are effective and easy are mentioned below. You can try different methods and then select the one that suits best to your body and fulfills its desired goals.

The 5:2 Diet Plan:

The first method for intermittent fasting is the 5:2 diet plan. This diet plan is about eating healthy 5 days a week and fasting for the rest of 2 days. Fasting here means to restrict calories to 500 per day only. This diet is also popular with the name "the Fast Diet" and it was first introduced by a British man Michael Mosely. It is reported that the 5:2 diet plan is one of the most effective ways of reducing weight and helps to get a better lifestyle. The 5:2 diet plan does not restrict you from the number of calories you intake. Or it is not about what foods are you eating. Unlike other diet plans like keto, etc., rather it focuses on the time of meals. So, it is better to say that the 5:2 diet plan is a plan that makes your lifestyle better and a healthy one.

It is said that women who are following a 5:2 diet plan should eat only 500 calories on fasting days, but a man should eat up to 600 calories. A man's body needs more calories to stay active. The best way to follow a 5:2 diet plan is to fast for two days of the week and eat the rest of the days except Mondays and Wednesdays. It is advised not to select consecutive days like Saturday Sunday but instead alternative days or you can select any two days according to your convenience.

The 5:2 diet plan is of no use if you are not doing it properly which is why below is a brief guide to the 5:2 diet plan of intermittent fasting.

How to do it?

The 5:2 diet plan is so simple to follow. In this intermittent fasting method, you have to fast for two days and can eat normally for the rest of the days. On fasting days, you can take a quarter of the total calories you consume on non-fasting days. It means the intake of 20-25% calories. It makes two small and healthy meals every fasting day.

Fasting for two days of the week does not mean you are free to eat everything for the rest of the days. Eating healthy is the main purpose of this diet plan. If you are eating junk and oily foods for the rest of the days you might lose no weight, instead, it will result in weight gain or some other health issues.

You can select any two days of the week, but it is better not to select consecutive days, as you might feel lazy or tired at the start. Some people face a little fatigued at the start of a 5:2 diet plan but it fades away when your body gets used to it.

Health Benefits Of 5:2 Diet plan:

The main purpose of the 5:2 diet plan is to gain all the health benefits hidden in intermittent fasting methods. Research and studies conducted on the 5:2 diet plans have confirmed that this method of intermittent fasting is good for health and has long-lasting effects on the human body. The most important health benefit of the 5:2 diet plan is the restriction of calories that results in weight loss and belly fats reduction, thus ensuring a healthy life ahead.

Let's find out the health benefits of 5:2 Diet plan:

Weight loss and belly fat reduction:

If you intend to lose weight then the 5:2 diet plan is surely one of the most effective ways of doing so. It is because the 5:2 diet plan helps to intake fewer calories in the fasting days and helps you shed extra body fats. The best thing about this diet plan is, you do not shed extra pounds suddenly. It is a slow and steady process that gives your body enough time to cooperate with new changes.

The research and studies conducted on the 5:2 diet plan have shown that it helps to reduce 4-8 percent of body weight in just a few weeks of fasting. It is an ideal weight loss plan if followed properly. The only thing that must be kept in mind while following the 5:2 diet plan is to eat healthy during the non-fasting days. Because if you are enjoying heavy fats and eating a lot of junk food like burgers, french fries, and other oily things, then there is no use of this diet plan.

It is recommended to take 2-3 small meals consisting of good fats, proteins, fibers, and calcium. A lot of nutritious food helps your body to stay active and fresh. Better eat some uncooked raw fruits and vegetables to get nutrients in their natural form. In addition to that, drinking a lot of water during both fasting and non-fasting days also helps in quick weight reduction. Also, water keeps the body hydrated and helps you perform in a better way.

The research and studies have found that the 5:2 method of intermittent fasting helps in:

- Reduction of 8% belly fats and extra weight in just 4-5 weeks of fasting.
- Reduction of a 4% waistline, indicating that the 5:2 diet plan is quite effective in reducing extra belly fats.
- Smaller reduction of muscular mass, as compared to all other weight control diet plans.
- Intermittent fasting becomes more effective if combined with some mild exercises like walking, etc.

Other health benefits:

Not only weight loss, intermittent fasting has many other health benefits listed as follows:

- This method of intermittent fasting helps in the control of blood sugar and regulates the insulin amount in the body.
- One research conducted on the 5:2 method of intermittent fasting has shown

that it resulted in weight loss similar to regular calorie restriction. Additionally, the diet was very effective at reducing insulin levels and helps to improve insulin sensitivity in the body.

- This diet plan is very effective for people who are suffering from some kind of heart disease or other allergies.

Different researches conducted on human body reveals that after fasting for 12 weeks or more the 5:2 diet plan of intermittent fasting results in

- Reduced body weight by more than 11 pounds that is equal to 5kgs. An idle weight loss for any individual for sure.
- Reduced fat mass by 7.7 pounds (3.5 kg), without a reduction in muscular mass.
- Decrease in blood levels of triglycerides by 20%.
- Improved LDL particle size, which is a good thing for the human body.

- Reduced levels of CRP, an important marker of inflammation. That indicates this method helps the body in fighting against inflammation.
- Reduced levels of leptin by up to 40%.

Risks Of 5:2 diet plan:

There is no doubt in the fact that intermittent fasting has a lot of health benefits. It helps the human body to function more properly and makes you healthy, wealthy and wise. But the 5:2 diet plan of intermittent fasting is not good for everyone. It does not benefit all human beings. Some people who have a medical history might feel some kind of side effects. The risks of intermittent fasting include diarrhea, severe headache, and weakness. Some individuals might feel constipation or irregular bowel movement because of nutrition's lack. That is why it is recommended to drink lots of water to avoid constipation.

The side effects of the 5:2 plans for women are different as compared to men. Women might face difficulties in periods, conceiving and pregnancy. The following are some side effects of intermittent fasting reported after several studies:

- · A lot of fatigue and laziness during fasting days.
- · Insufficient nutrient intake might leave you tired all day.
- · Eating disorders like eating a lot of food in the non-fasting days.
- · Food cravings all the time may distract you from your daily life works.
- · Women might feel irregular periods or no periods at all.
- · Low sugar level for diabetic patients.

You might feel laziness and fatigue at the start of fasting days, but usually, it gets normal with time. Health experts suggest keeping yourself busy with tasks that do not take much energy like watching a movie, listening to songs or talking to friends or colleagues.

If you are practicing 5:2 diet plan of intermittent fasting, and facing any of the above side effects, you are recommended to stop fasting for a few weeks and get yourself checked as soon as possible.

Following individuals should avoid the 5:2 method of intermittent fasting:

- People having any medical history like diabetes, and heart disease, underweight boys and girls.
- Individuals with a history of eating disorders.
- Breastfeeding and pregnant women or women who are trying to conceive.

- People suffering from anxiety or any other psychological disorder.

The 5:2 diet plan is the best method to lose weight but consult your doctor first before starting it.

What to eat during 5:2 method of intermittent fasting:

Though intermittent fasting does not limit you to what to eat and how to eat but it focuses on the time you are eating plus the main focus is on eating healthy. Eating healthy is not about quitting your favorite dishes or eating one or two things only, eating healthy means your food intake should fulfill the body requirements of all vitamins and nutrition. So on the non-fasting days, you can eat everything that is healthy it could be fruits vegetables, meat, fish, nuts, food cooked in olive oil, avocados, lentils, low sugar drinks and coffee and a lot of water to keep yourself hydrated, just make sure your food intake is enough to keep your body healthy and strong.

On the contrary, on fasting days, the 5:2 diet plan demands to limit calories to 500-600. It makes 25% of total calorie intake. 500 calories are idle for women, while men need around 600 calories. Though there is no hard and fast rule about when to eat on the fasting days, different people follow different plans according to their convenience. Some individuals like to start the day with a light breakfast and a cup of coffee while others concentrate on eating during lunch or supper time.

The following two diet plans are idle for fasting days.

- 3 small meals consisting of a light breakfast, supper, and lunch.
- 2 fine meals consisting of lunch and a very light dinner only.

The following foods are best for fasting days as they are enriched in vitamins and nutrition. They give the body certain energy and keeps you active while fasting.

- A generous portion of vegetables
- Natural yogurt with berries
- Boiled eggs. You can also have scrambled or baked eggs.
- Grilled fish like salmon or lean meat
- Cauliflower rice
- Soups.
- Low-calorie cup soups
- Black coffee.
- Low sugar tea
- A lot of water.

Here is a brief guideline to follow the 5:2 method of intermittent and get complete benefits out of it.

The 16/8 method:

It is one of the very effective ways of intermittent fasting and helps you lose weight very quickly. The 16/8 Method includes fasting each day for 14 to16 hours and confining your day by "eating window" to 8-10 hours. Inside the eating window, you can fit in 2, 3, or more suppers. But the suppers must include a healthy diet. I am going to discuss what a healthy diet should consist of.

This technique is otherwise called the Leangains convention and was promoted by very famous health expert Martin Berkhan. Doing this technique for fasting can really be as basic as not having anything after supper and skipping breakfast. For instance, in the event that you finish your last supper at 8 p.m. what's more, if you do not eat until early afternoon the following day, you're in fact fasting for 16 hours.

It is, for the most part, suggested that ladies just quick 14-15 hours, since they appear to improve marginally shorter fasts. It is also important to remember that for individuals who get ravenous toward the beginning of the day and like to have breakfast, this technique might be difficult to follow since morning.

Fasting does not mean to skip all the liquids as well. You can drink water, espresso, and other non-caloric refreshments during the fasting period which can help decrease sentiments of appetite and give you some energy to survive throughout the day.

It is critical to principally eat well nourishments during your eating window. This strategy won't work on the off chance that you eat bunches of low-quality nourishment or eating fast foods like chips, oily foods, burgers or any other food that is rich in calories.

Let's talk about the 16/8 fasting method in detail.

How to do it?

The easiest way to do the 16/8 method of intermittent fasting is to find a perfect 16 hours fasting window for yourself. Many health experts advise to include sleeping hours in the fasting time, so it would become easy for you to sustain the fats. Moreover, in the opinion of many doctors and researchers, it has been proved that eating earlier in the evening helps in the food digestion process and proper calories burning procedure. Many researchers conducted intermittent fasting which has proved that the human body has a fast digestion process while awake. During sleep, the digestion process slows down hence the extra body fats do not burn out in proper manner.

Though some people might not be able to consume their food at 6 pm in the evening. They are recommended to have their last meal 3-4 hours prior to sleep. Every human body has a different reaction to the 16/8 intermittent fasting method. Though there is not any hard and fast rule to include sleep hours in the fast timing it is the better way suggested by doctors and health experts.

You can choose your fasting hours according to your convenience from the 3 option given below:

- 9 a.m. to 5 p.m.

- 10 a.m. to 6 p.m.
- Noon to 8 p.m.

Some people need to experiment before selecting the best eating window for them. Therefore, if you have recently started intermittent fasting 16/8 method, try it for a few weeks and then decide which eating window is best and convenient for you.

People can have snacks and fluids during their fasting hours. Intermittent fasting experts allow having 25 percent of total calories during the fasting time if you are feeling lazy or finding it difficult to continue your fats.

Recommended foods during 16/8 fasting method:

Unlike other diet plans like keto diet etc., intermittent fasting does not limit the intake of calories. Instead, all the health experts have stressed on taking healthy meals while breaking fast and during the eating window. Consuming a lot of junk foods or oily foods may not support you in getting the desired benefits of intermittent fasting. Health experts suggest taking healthy meals that include proteins, carbohydrates, fats, and fibers. I have listed down a few healthy meals that you should take while practicing intermittent fasting.

- Lots of raw fruits and vegetables. They can be fresh or frozen. Raw fruits and veggies are rich in proteins and fibers and give the body a new strength and power to sustain fasting. Also, it helps to avoid the possible side effects of intermittent fasting like nausea, headache, body collapse, and others.

- A lot of whole grains including brown rice, oats, and barley. Whole grains are also protein-enriched foods.
- Eat other protein-enriched foods like poultry, fish, beans, lentils, tofu, nuts, seeds, low-fat cottage cheese, and eggs. (eggs could be taken in any form boil or scrambled eggs)
- Good fats like avocados, olive oil, salmon fish, nuts, coconuts, and seeds.

Drinking low-fat beverages also helps in sustaining the fast. It is recommended that people practicing intermittent fasting should drink a lot of water and some low sugary beverages that help them to stay hydrated and active. A lot of times, people confuse thirst with hunger as well. So, drinking enough water helps them in fighting hunger too.

The following are some useful tips for the people practicing intermittent fasting 16/8 method. These things might help you in getting the desired benefit out of intermittent fasting.

- Drinking cinnamon tea during fasting hours helps in reducing hunger and gives the body some energy.
- Drink a lot of water throughout the day. 14 glasses of water are the ideal consumption.
- Do not watch YouTube videos or food images. It might stimulate your hunger.
- As exercise can trigger hunger, that is why it is recommended to exercise during the eating window. Walking along with intermittent fasting has a significant impact.
- Try some useful meditation while fasting. Like listening to some music or watching movies to reduce hunger.

Risks Of 16/8 intermittent fasting method:

It is to tell you that the 16/8 method of intermittent fasting is not for everyone. It involves some risks and side effects on human health. It is to advise that before starting this method of intermittent fasting it is better to concern your doctor. Special for women intermittent fasting might have an impact on women's fertility and body communication with ovaries. So, if you have any plan to start intermittent fasting, do not do it without consulting a pro.

The following are some of the risk factors involved in the 16/8 method of intermittent fasting.

- At the beginning of this method, you might feel an intense hunger feeling. Tiredness, dizziness, and headache. It is because of longer fasting hours. Once the body gets used to it, these feelings become normal.
- · It might develop some eating disorder habits in some individuals. As intense hunger forces humans to eat whatever they find. Eating a lot of junk food might be a result of the 16/8 method.
- · Overeating might lead you toward severe acid reflux or heartburn.

People undergoing some medical problems, like underweight women, people suffering from any kind of mental or eating disorder and pregnant women should start the 16/8 method after doctor's consultation.

Also, this 16:8 method of intermittent fasting is not good for people who have anxiety and depression. Fasting might make this depression intense. Adults of ager 50 years or plus should not start intermittent fasting on their own. Get yourself properly checked before taking any kind of decision.

Benefits of the 16/8 method of intermittent fasting:

Though intermittent fasting has a lot of benefits on human health, all the methods of intermittent fasting have some positive impacts on human health. The following are some of the health benefits of the 16/8 method of intermittent fasting.

Prevention Against diseases:

Intermittent fasting has a lot of benefits. It provokes a healthy lifestyle as well as prevents the body from many chronic diseases. Method16/8 of intermittent fasting has many proven health benefits as well as it prepares the human body to fight against many other diseases and makes the immune system stronger. According to some health experts and intermittent fasting supporters, this method helps the body to fight against the following diseases.

- type 2 diabetes
- better heart health
- Fight against certain types of cancer.
- neurodegenerative illnesses

Although there have been numerous studies and researches related to the 16:8 method and its benefits on health, many areas are still undiscovered. A 2014 audit reports that intermittent fasting shows that this method of intermittent fasting limits down the calorie intake and helps in insulin reduction levels in the blood. In addition to that, it controls blood sugar levels (mostly in men) and thus it helps the human body to fight against type 2 diabetes. Though there is still some room for more investigation, a lot more information about the prevention of diseases is still to come. A recent report demonstrates that not only this method of intermittent fasting is helpful in weight reduction, but also an 8-hour eating window may help decrease circulatory strain in adults and all other individuals.

Different investigations report that intermittent fasting lessens fasting glucose by 3–6% in those with prediabetes, despite the fact that it has no impact on people who already have regular blood sugar levels. It might diminish fasting insulin by 11–57% following 3 to 24 weeks of intermittent fasting. Fasting methods like 16:8 hours fasting may have a strong influence on the cerebrum and thus improve the human learning process as well. The people who are practicing this method have also shown better memory skills and according to the reports, this fasting method is helpful in brain cell development. According to some research and studies on intermittent fasting in 2017, it has been reported that this method of fasting also prevents the body against nonalcoholic greasy liver sickness and malignant growth.

Extended Life Span:

Many researchers conducted on animals have shown that this method of intermittent fasting has positive impacts on life span. It has been observed that the animals fasting for 16 hours have a longer life span as compared to the one that does not. Different creature examination recommend that intermittent fasting may support creatures with living longer. For instance, one examination found that transient continued fasting expanded the life expectancy of female mice. The National Institute on Aging points out that, though there already have been so much researches on the effects on intermittent fasting on life span but despite everything we can't clarify why fasting stretches life expectancy. Human investigations in the region are constrained, and the potential advantages of intermittent fasting for human life span are not yet known.

Weight loss:

It has been stated that eating for 8 hours window reduces the number of calories that the human body is taking in. In addition to that, 16 hours fast may help to boost a certain level of metabolic rate and thus helps in a fast weight loss process. Fasting for 16 hours helps the stored belly fats to be burned and yet result in a reduction of belly fats which might be a cause of weight increase. Many researchers conducted on the human body have shown that this method of fasting helps in quicker fat reduction as compared to all other diet plans. Research from 2016 reports that men who followed a 16:8 approach for 8 weeks while fighting training showed a reduction in fat mass. The participants maintained their muscle mass throughout. Interestingly, a recent report discovered next to no distinction in weight reduction between members who rehearsed intermittent fasting as alternate day fasting instead of 16:8 fasting. Moreover, the individuals who decreased their general calorie consumption. The dropout rate was likewise high among those who are practicing intermittent fasting for a few weeks.

Precisely it is safe to say that this method of intermittent fasting has more effect on fat and weight loss as compared to all other methods. One thing that should be kept in mind, that if you are not healthy while eating, the weight loss process would not be the same.

Eat Stop Eat:

This method of intermittent fasting is not for soft-hearted people. In my point of view, it is the toughest of all, but as we all know hard work always pays off. So, it is surely an effective one. This method is about fasting for 24 hours once or twice a week. The other 5 days you can eat normally. This method was discovered by Brad Pilon and until now it is one of most famous and effective diet methods. Eat stop eat requires you to fast from lunch-lunch, breakfast-breakfast or dinner to dinner to complete 24 hours. For instance, you have had your dinner at 8 pm one night, so do not eat any solid food until next night. This is not an easy job for everyone. You can also start it with 12-14 hours fast and then increase the fasting hours slowly. Drinking water or other low-fat juices are fine during fasting. It gives you the energy to sustain the fast.

Eat stop eat is an effective fasting plan that helps to reduce the weight in less time. If you are worried about increasing weight, this method is surely going to help you. But make sure you are supposed to eat healthy for the rest of 5 days as well. Ignore fast foods, oily foods, and sugary drinks. We can say that eat stop eat is not your typical diet plan. It is different from all other diet plans like keto and etc. it is better to say that it just reschedules your mealtime. We grew up listening to fact that there are 3 meals a day. Do breakfast like a king, have supper like a prince and eat dinner like a pauper. Though breakfast is a very important meal of the day, I am not denying this fact but on the other hand, skipping breakfast or any other meal for the sake of intermittent fasting is beneficial for human health. Eat stop eat method wants you to quit some of your meals and help you in rescheduling your meal timings.

This method of intermittent fasting is getting very famous around the world. A lot of people around the globe are practicing this method and they are getting the desired results. But there is no use of this method if not done properly. There are dos and don'ts of eat stop eat method that everyone must know.

Although this method is a bit hectic and useful still it is very important to do it in the right manner. Here's a brief guide to Eat stop eat method of intermittent fasting:

How to do it?

The application of the eat stop eat method is not difficult at all. It is a straight forward fasting plan that requires you to select any one or two days of the week and fast for 24 hours. For the rest of the days, you can have your normal diet.

It is to assure that the two days you are selecting are not consecutive. It could be Monday and Thursday or Tuesday and Friday. Depending upon your convenience. Eat stop eat method involves fasting from meal to meal. Following are the three fasting plans from which you can select the best one for yourself.

- Fasting from breakfast to breakfast.
- Fasting from lunch to lunch.
- Fasting from dinner to dinner.

There is no hard and fast rule that you have to obey. Just learn how your body works while following the above three different fasting plans and choose the one that suits best to your fasting requirements.

Keeping in mind, avoid the extra calories and heavy feasts during non-fasting days. Eat as much that is sufficient for your body. Overeating or eating unhealthily would have an adverse effect on your body. In addition to that, on fasting days make sure your body is well hydrated. Many people do not drink enough water and feel tired and lazy all the time. Make sure you are taking 14 glasses of water every day. Low sugary beverages also prevent fatigue and keep your body hydrated and active while fasting.

Eat stop eat is the fasting method that affects different human bodies in different manners.

Researches and studies have shown that this method of intermittent fasting for weight loss is 10% effective on the different individuals. Though we can't predict its possible results on anyone before applying it over a human body.

Health Benefits of Eat Stop Eat:

Eat stop eat fasting method has a lot of health benefits. It is stated that it affects man and woman bodies in different manners. Let's find out the health benefits of eating.

Weight loss:

Most of the people following the eat stop eat method to lose extra body fats and calories. This method is quite useful in weight loss and helps in the burning of extra calories and belly fats in the fasting days. Our body needs 3500 calories to work in a proper manner. The rest of the calories remains in the body in the shape of fats and thus results in weight gain. There is no better way to consume those extra belly fats other than fasting for longer time periods. During the time of fasting, as the body is taking in no more calories, the previous calories are being burned and give the energy to sustain. Losing weight requires you to take fewer calories than you are burning. That is why it is important to avoid heavy feasts during the non-fasting days as well.

When the eat stop eat method is followed in a proper manner the calorie intake reduces to zero in the fasting days that might result in quick weight loss just in a few weeks. Well, the currents studies and researches haven't shown that restricting calories for an entire day at a time is any more effective for reducing weight than the continual daily calorie restriction.

Change In body Metabolism:

Eat stop eat method might show up some changes in the human metabolic rate. According to some health experts, change in metabolic rate also helps in weight reduction and reduces belly fats and stored calories. Another way Eat Stop Eat could prompt weight reduction is a direct result of certain metabolic movements that happen when your body is in a fasted state. The body's favored fuel source is carbs. At the point when you eat carbs, there are separated into a usable type of vitality known as glucose. After around 12–36 hours of fasting, the vast majority will consume the glucose they have put away in their bodies and in this way change to utilizing fat as a vitality source. This is a metabolic state known as ketosis.

Early research proposes that as a result of this metabolic move, intermittent fasting may support fat use. Other weight control strategies and diet plans do not support this cause any better than fasting for a few weeks. In any case, information on this potential advantage is constrained, and there is by all account's critical changeability in how rapidly individuals progress into ketosis.

In this way, it is far-fetched that everybody will arrive at ketosis inside the 24-hour fasting window utilized in the Eat Stop Eat diet. Though there has been already so much work done on effects of intermittent fasting on human health, still more research is expected to see how metabolic changes that may happen on an Eat Stop Eat diet can impact fat decrease and generally speaking weight reduction methods.

Side Effects of Eat Stop Eat Method:

Though there are many health benefits of the eat stop eat method and all of the above it is best for calorie control and weight reduction but it is important to mention that this fasting method is not suitable for everyone. Every human body has different capabilities and patience levels. Different human bodies react in different ways of eating. That is why it is recommended to consult a doctor before starting to stop eating intermittent fasting. Following people should not start this method of fasting without doctor's consultation.

- Pregnant women.
- Breastfeeding women.
- Women who are trying to conceive.
- People suffering from anxiety or depression or any other physic disorder.

- Underweight people.
- People having any kind of eating disorders.
- People with weak immune systems.

Eat stop eat method might have some side effects on the human body. If you are facing any of the following effects it is recommended to stop intermittent fasting right away and get yourself properly checked.

Insufficient Nutrition:

People who are following the eat stop eat fasting routine must pay a lot of attention to the food they are eating on non-fasting days. It is important to take all the nutritious foods to keep your body active and strong. Many individuals just focus on how many hours they are fasting and how much weight is lost without paying attention to the nutritious needs of the body. The food we eat is just not calories. It is a composition of vitamins, proteins, calcium, fibers, carbohydrates, and fats. And if you are consuming less nutrition you may feel laziness, fatigue and might feel hungry all the time.

Make a proper diet plan for non-fasting days and eat healthy meals to properly fulfill your body needs.

Low Level of blood sugar:

Intermittent fasting is one of the best ways to control blood sugar levels and to regulate insulin in the body. But as I have mentioned already fasting might have a different impact on different individuals. Some people might not face any problem regarding their blood sugar level and they keep on going, while others might face low levels of sugar and feel drowsiness. As eat stop eat method of intermittent fasting might result in the limited intake of calories that has an impact on the level of sugar in the blood.

Especially the people who are suffering from any kind of medical problem such as diabetes might suffer severe low sugar levels. In case of any medical issue or severe low sugar level, it is advised to see the doctor as soon as possible. Moreover, stop fasting right away and eat something healthy.

Hormonal Changes:

Eat stop eat method of intermittent fasting might lead the body towards a certain kind of hormonal changes. According to some research, it is said that intermittent fasting might affect the metabolic rate of the body that has a further impact on human hormones. Different individuals have shown different hormonal reactions after intermittent fasting. The studies have shown intermittent fasting is beneficial for some women as it improves fertility. Whereas there are some opposite reactions as well such as irregular and missed periods and certain kinds of problems that might lead to pregnancy and conceiving complications.

There is not any final verdict on how the human body hormones will behave while intermittent fasting because of the mixed data and limited total evidence. Eat Stop Eat is not generally recommended for anyone who's pregnant, breastfeeding, or doing efforts to conceive. In addition to that person who is underweight and is fighting with depression should not start intermittent fasting

If you have a history of hormonal dysregulation, irregular periods, or amenorrhea, consult your healthcare provider before starting to eat stop eat intermittent fasting. Otherwise, it might lead you towards some severe health problems.

Psychology Impact of Eat stop Eat method:

Though fasting is safe for many healthy individuals. It is reported that fasting improves brain cells' activity and helps in better memory as well. Some people feel extremely good and physiological changes and good mood swings have been reported. But researches have also shown that eat stop eat method of intermittent fasting can also lead you towards some negative physiological disorder and they might be dangerous.

Some individuals have reported that all these mood issues get resolved once you get used to the fasting routine. It might be true but researchers and doctors haven't confirmed this claim yet. Intermittent fasting might trigger your food cravings and you end up thinking about the food all the time. That is why the stop eats method of intermittent fasting is not recommended for anyone who has a history of eating disorder or any other psychological disorder. It is suggested to concern your health expert in any of the above cases and get the proper treatment done.

The Warrior Method: Fast during Day and Eating at Night:

Another method of intermittent fasting is to fast during the day and eat a huge amount of meals during the night. This method of fasting was introduced by a very famous health expert named Ori Hofmekler and it has been a very good help on reducing weight quickly. This fasting method requires you to eat some raw fruit and vegetables during the day time and eat one good healthy processed meal at night. This method is an easy way for beginners who are trying to lose weight but in an easy manner. As the name suggests this diet plan has got some inspiration from the ancient warriors. The warriors back then used to eat a little amount of food during the day time and eat good healthy foods at night in order to fulfill the body's nutritional requirements and to stay healthy and active.

This diet plan mainly focuses on fasting for 20 hours a day, by fasting here means you can have small meals during the day time, like eating raw fruits, or dairy products like milk and boiled eggs and after complete 24 hours, eat as much as you want but eat healthy meals consist up of all the proteins and vitamins. In the beginning, it is recommended to start a 3-4-week plan. Continue if you to accept it and you are getting positive results. The warrior diet plan is one effective way of weight loss and in addition to that, it has several health benefits if followed properly. Let's find the dos and don'ts of the warrior diet plan in detail.

So, here is all you need to know about the warrior diet.

How to do it?

Hofmekler has suggested that anyone who is planning to start a warrior diet should follow it for3 weeks first. It is the 3-phase plan that helps to improve the body ability and energy. Following is the 3 weeks plan for the beginners.

Detox (week 1)
· Under eat for 20 hours during the day on vegetable juices, clear stock, dairy (yogurt, curds), hard-bubbled eggs and crude foods grown from the ground.

• During the four-hour eating period, eat a serving of mixed greens with oil and vinegar dressing, trailed by one huge or various dinners of plant proteins (beans), sans wheat entire grains, modest quantities of cheddar and cooked vegetables.

• Espresso, tea, water and limited quantities of milk can be devoured for the duration of the day.

High fat (week 2)
• Under eat for 20 hours during the day on vegetable juices, clear soup, dairy (yogurt, curds), hard-bubbled eggs and crude foods grown from the ground.

• During the four-hour eating period at night, eat a serving of mixed greens with oil and vinegar dressing, trailed by lean creature protein, cooked vegetables and in any event one bunch of nuts.

· No grains or starches are devoured during week 2.

Concluding fat loss (week 3)

This week's plan focuses on high protein and high carbs intake. It has several cycles.

- 1–2 days high in carbs
- 1–2 days high in protein and low in carbs
- 1–2 days high in carbs
- Vice versa.

Now, here is what you should eat during these cycles. On high carbs day, the following food intake is suggested to get the best results.

- Under eat for 20 hours during the day on vegetable juices, clear juices, dairy (yogurt, curds), hard-bubbled eggs and crude foods grown from the ground.

- During the four-hour eating window eat a serving of mixed greens with oil and vinegar dressing, trailed by cooked vegetables, a certain amount of protein intake along with primary starch, for example, corn, potatoes, pasta or grains.

On the other hand, in the days of high protein cycles, the following meal plan is suggested to get the best results.

- Restrict eating for 20 hours during the day on vegetable juices, clear stock, dairy (yogurt, curds), hard-bubbled eggs and crude products of the soil.

- During the four-hour eating window at night, eat a serving of mixed greens with oil and vinegar dressing, trailed by 8–16 ounces of creature protein with a side of cooked, non-bland vegetables.

- In spite of the fact that grains or starches are not to be eaten during the week 3 indulging window, a modest quantity of crisp tropical organic products can be eaten for dessert.

Health benefits of the warrior Diet:

Since the warrior diet plan is tougher than all other plans of intermittent fasting, but it is very effective and has a lot of health benefits. Let's find out the health benefits of the warrior diet plan.

Weight loss:

It is one of the most effective and useful ways to shed some extra body pounds and belly fats. It has been proved that the warrior diet plan is one of the effective ways of weight loss as compared to other calorie-restricted diet plans. Recent research conducted on the impact of the warrior diet stated that various types of intermittent fasting, ranging from 3 to 12 months, were more effective at promoting weight loss as compared to any other diet plan. As the warrior method restricts the food intake for several hours, thus the reduction and consumption of extra belly fats take place that further results in reduced weight and waistline.

Fights inflammation:

Though inflammation has a lot of health benefits it prevents the body against certain disease but at the same time, acute inflammation can lead to serious health consequences. According to some research done, chronic inflammation can lead the human body towards dangerous diseases including heart disease, some types of cancer and arthritis. Fasting helps the human body to fight against chronic inflammation.

A research conducted on 50 people found that those fasting for the Muslim holiday of Ramadan had significantly lower levels of the inflammatory protein (CRP) and homocysteine. As compared to the individuals who do not fast for even a single day.

Improved Brain Health:

The Warrior Diet is promoted as a way to improve brain health. many types of research and studies conducted on this method of intermittent fasting have already shown that fasting makes the human brain better and helps in cell growth. Intermittent fasting has been found to benefit the regulation of inflammatory pathways that affect your brain function. For example, animal studies have shown that intermittent fasting reduced inflammatory markers like interleukin 6 (IL-6) and tumor necrosis factor-alpha (TNF-α), which may negatively impact memory and learning. Thus, fasting helps in better memory and learning. Other animal studies found that intermittent fasting has a protective effect against Alzheimer's disease

Risks of the Warrior diet plan:

Though this method if intermittent fasting has many health benefits. But at the same time, it can lead your body towards certain health issues if not followed properly. Many individuals have different reactions to the warrior diet, and they might feel the following side effects.

- Fatigue
- Dizziness
- Low energy

- Lightheadedness

- Anxiety

- Insomnia

- Extreme hunger

- Low blood sugar

- Constipation

- Fainting

- Irritability

- Hormonal imbalance

- Weight gain

Some of the above side effects vanish as the body gets used to the new fasting method, but in case of any severe reaction, it is recommended to stop fasting at the moment and get proper medical health.

What to eat during the warrior diet plan?

Although the warrior diet does not limit the intake of calories at the time when you are not fasting, still it is very important to make healthy meals in the non-fasting hours. All the health experts and doctors have suggested the following things to eat in the non-fasting hours, to keep your body healthy and fresh. And to get all the benefits out of the warrior diet plan.

- A lot of raw fruits including apples, bananas, kiwi, mango, peach, pineapple, etc.
- Vegetable juices: Beet, carrots, cucumber and also raw vegetables
- The broth of any meat you like could be beef and chicken broth.
- Condiments: Small amounts of olive oil, apple cider vinegar, etc.
- Dairy: Milk, yogurt, cottage cheese, etc.
- Protein: Hard-boiled or poached eggs or scrambled eggs.
- Cooked vegetables: Cauliflower, brussels sprouts, zucchini, greens, etc.

- Proteins: Chicken, steak, fish, turkey, eggs, etc.
- Starches: beans, potatoes, corn, sweet potatoes, etc.
- Grains: Oats, quinoa, pasta, bread, barley, etc.
- Fats: Nuts, olive oil, etc.
- Beverages: a lot of water, coffee, tea, etc.

The above-mentioned food and fruits are full of vitamins, minerals, proteins, fibers, and good fats. The composition of all this food will help you to stay happy and healthy. On the other hand, there are certain unhealthy foods that should be avoided during the warrior diet. As they can leave some negative impacts and you might not get the desired results.

- Candy
- Cookies and cakes
- Chips
- Fast food including burgers, pizza's and oily food

- Fried foods
- Processed meats (lunch meats, bacon)
- Artificial or refined carbohydrates
- Artificial sweeteners
- Sweetened drinks like fruit juice.

Alternate Day Fasting:

Alternate day fasting as the name suggests is the fasting method that requires a 24-hours fast every alternate day. This method is not recommended for beginners as it is not an easy one. If you want to lose weight and improve body metabolism then alternate day fasting is a good choice. On fasting day, you are only allowed to intake 500-600 calories along with some low-fat juices, coffee and a lot of water.

It is very important to do alternative fasting in the right manner. So below is a brief guide to alternate-day fasting.

How to do it?

The basic idea of this fasting technique is to fast every next day. You can eat for one day and fast for the other. On a non-fasting day, it is recommended to take 3 proper meals as your normal routine. These meals should be healthy and full of nutrition. But on the fasting day, the calorie intake is limited to 25%. You can have two small meals including a small breakfast (an egg with black coffee) and a small dinner (some vegetables) along with a lot of water out the day.

Health benefit of Alternate-day Fasting:

Researches and studies have shown alternate day fasting has a lot of positive health impacts. Some Important benefits of this fasting method are mentioned below.

Type 2 Diabetes:

Type 2 diabetes represents 90–95% of diabetes cases in the United States Furthermore, more than 33% of Americans have prediabetes, a condition wherein glucose levels are higher than ordinary yet not sufficiently high to be viewed as diabetes Getting thinner and confining calories is typically a compelling method to improve or turn around numerous side effects of type 2 diabetes.

Also, to nonstop calorie limitation, ADF appears to cause mellow decreases in chance elements for type 2 diabetes among individuals who are overweight. In addition to that, ADF appears to be best at decreasing insulin levels and insulin opposition, while just minutely affecting glucose the executives

Having high insulin levels, or hyperinsulinemia has been connected to heftiness and ceaseless maladies, for example, coronary illness and malignant growth

Among people with prediabetes, 8–12 weeks of ADF have been shown to diminish fasting insulin by around 20-31%. That is quite good. A decrease in insulin levels and insulin obstruction should prompt a fundamentally diminished danger of type 2 diabetes, particularly when joined with weight reduction.

Weight loss:

Like all other methods of intermittent fasting, alternate-day fasting is also one of the effective methods for weight loss. Alternate day fasting limits the calorie intake up to 25% only the fasting day that helps in weight reduction. Reducing extra belly fat helps the body to remain healthy and active for a longer period of time. Weight reduction also results in a better life span and prevents the body against many chronic diseases.

Heart Health:

Heart diseases are one of the leading causes of death around the world. Every day hundreds of people die because of heart failure. The basic reason behind these deaths is either heart attack or increased levels of bad cholesterol in the blood. Researchers have proved that fasting is one of the best ways to control heart health and to make it better. When a human body fasts for hours, it results in the burning of bad fats and thus keeps the heart and body healthy.

Alternate fasting is one of the most effective ways of improved heart health. One study comprises of overweight and obese people shows that after 8-12 weeks of alternate-day fasting following changes have been seen in their bodies.

- Reduced waist circumference up to 2–2.8 inches or 5–7 cm.
- Decreased blood pressure and control blood sugar especially in men.
- Lowered LDL (bad) cholesterol the reduced level of cholesterol is up to 20–25%.
- Increase in number of large LDL particles and reduced number of dangerous small, dense LDL particles

- Decreased blood triglycerides up to 30%.

Autophagy:

One of the most well-known impacts of fasting is the incitement of autophagy. Autophagy is a procedure wherein old pieces of cells are corrupted and reused. It assumes a key job in forestalling ailments, including malignant growth, neurodegeneration, coronary illness, and diseases

Creature contemplates have reliably indicated that long-and transient fasting increment autophagy and are connected to postponed maturing and a decreased danger of tumors

Besides, fasting has been appeared to expand life expectancy in rodents, flies, yeasts, and worms in addition, cell considers have demonstrated that fasting invigorates autophagy, bringing about impacts that may help keep you sound and live more.

This has been affirmed by human examinations demonstrating that ADF slims down lessen oxidative harm and advance changes that might be connected to life span the discoveries look exceptionally encouraging, yet the impacts of ADF on autophagy and life span should be concentrated all the more broadly.

What to eat During Alternate Day fasting?

There is no hard and fast rule regarding what to eat on fasting days. The one thing that you should keep in mind is to limit the calories intake up to 500 -600 only. On the non-fasting days feel free to enjoy all the healthy meals.

The best thing is to drink low sugary drinks on fasting days like black coffee, tea and a lot of water to stay hydrated and active. Remember that if you are not taking enough water, dehydration can lead you toward many severe health risks.

Many people prefer to take 500 calories at once on the fasting day. It depends on your convenience. You can also divide them into 2 meals or take 1 large meal consisting of 25% of total calories. The following are some suitable meals for fasting days.

- Eggs and vegetables
- Yogurt with berries
- Grilled fish or lean meat with vegetables
- Soup and a piece of fruit
- A green leafy salad with meat.

Risks of alternate-day fasting:

Though this method of intermittent fasting has many health benefits. But at the same time, it can lead your body towards certain health issues if not followed properly. Many individuals have different reactions to alternate-day fasting, and they might feel the following side effects.

- Fatigue
- Dizziness
- Low energy
- Lightheadedness
- Anxiety
- Insomnia
- Extreme hunger
- Low blood sugar
- Constipation
- Fainting
- Irritability

- Hormonal imbalance
- Weight gain

Some of the above side effects vanish as the body gets used to the new fasting method, but in case of any severe reaction, it is recommended to stop fasting at the moment and get proper medical health.

The above methods are best when it comes to intermittent fasting. But they may involve some health risk if you are not following them in a proper way. Everything needs to be done in a proper manner. Fasting is not a joke at all, it might lead you towards some health risk if you are not taking it seriously. So, I am going to write down how to fast safely to avoid all the health risks associated with fasting.

Some useful tips to fast safely:

Here are some useful tips to fast safely. Let's have a look at them.

Drink a lot of water:

Fasting for a long period of time might result in dehydration, headaches, dry lips and throats and fatigue. So, the best way to avoid all these things is to drink a lot of water and keep yourself hydrated. According to some health experts, it is important to drink 2-3 liters of water every day (14 glasses of water) otherwise there might be a risk of body collapse.

As 20-30% of water comes from food while fasting your body is already missing this percentage of water. Health experts suggest drinking coffee and some other healthy low-fat juices during fasting to avoid the risk of dehydration. Also, it helps you to sustain fasting in a more effective way.

Eat a small amount of food:

If you are a beginner, it is safe to take 500-600 calories during fasting days. Although fasting means to quit all kinds of solid food, taking 25% calories per day is safe and it prevents you from body collapse at once. It is better to intake raw foods like fruits and vegetables. Eat them likewise without processing and they will give you some energy to sustain the fast.

Do not break the fast with huge meals:

After the long hours of fasting, everyone wants to have one great meal that includes all your favorite dishes. But breaking a fast with a great feast is not a good idea at all. Eating heavy and unhealthy food after fasting may lead you towards dizziness and you might feel tired. It will make your body inactive. And it would not help you in the weight loss process as well. Instead try to make healthy meals that have good proteins, fats, and fibers. Fibers help in weight reduction and keep you healthy and active. So, it is suggested to keep your diet normal after breaking the fast.

Go for Walk:

Avoid eating requires getting your mind distracted. Distract your mind by doing some activities that do not involve a lot of energy. Like walking and meditating. Go for a walk in the evening or in the morning. Try to keep yourself busy, observe nature and distract your mind away. Or you can read a book with a glass of juice in hand, listen to music or watch your favorite movie to spend quality time.

Break the fast if not feeling well:

Breaking the fast is not a sin when it comes to your life. Yes, nothing is more important than life itself. So, if you are feeling dizziness, dehydration or feel like your body is going to collapse, break the fast. Sometimes staying hungry for longer periods of time makes you nauseated or weak. In this situation, it is okay to break a fast by eating something healthy and nutritious.

Seek medical help if important or consider some food supplements too.

Fasting is not for everyone:

Though fasting is good for health, it does not mean every person can do every kind of fasting.

Before fasting, it is important to study and observe your body. Or to consult some health experts or doctors.

Avoid Fasting if:

- People who have problems with blood or sugar regulations.
- People with low blood pressure
- Those who are taking prescription medications
- Woman with a history of amenorrhea
- Older adults
- Adolescents
- People with a medical condition like heart disease or type 2 diabetes
- Women who are trying to conceive a baby.
- Women who are pregnant
- People who are underweight
- Women who are breastfeeding.

Take Supplements:

Fasting regularly might make you a little lazy or weak. Fasting for long hours means you miss out on a lot of nutrition and vitamins. So, it is advised to take some supplements after consulting with your health expert or doctor.

Especially for the people who are fasting for weight loss, it is important for you to take some multivitamins. Multivitamins would help you to maintain your regular body strength.

Eat whole foods when not fasting:

The main purpose of fasting is to improve your health and to stay active. Despite the fact that fasting includes going without nourishment, it is as essential to keep up a whole food on days when you are not fasting. Whole food regimens dependent on entire nourishments are connected to a wide scope of medical advantages, including a diminished danger of malignancy, coronary illness, and other ceaseless diseases.

You can ensure you're eating good meals and stay sound by picking entire nourishments like meat, fish, eggs, vegetables, foods grown from the ground when you eat.

Precisely we can say that if fasting is done the right away, it can have many positive effects on the human body. Also, it is important to make healthy meals in a day when you are not fasting. So here I am going to tell you what a healthy meal is that you should consume on a daily basis.

Healthy meals to sustain a Healthy Lifestyle:

Healthy meals mean foods that are enriched with lots of nutrition, fibers, good fats, calcium and minerals. That keeps your body active and healthy. All these foods are human-friendly and have a lot of health benefits if taken in a proper proportion. The healthy meals mentioned below should be part of your daily diet.

Fruits and Vegetables:

Fruits and Vegetables are the best combinations of all the important minerals, calcium, protein and fibers that you should take in your daily meals. All fruits and vegetables are enriched with a lot of vitamins that not only keep you healthy but also very active and prevent your body against all the again effects.

It is suggested to take a full plate of fruits and veggies on a daily basis. Keep a fresh carrot or cucumber in your pocket or bag and eat it whenever you are hungry.

There is no food better than freshly home-grown fruits and vegetables.

Low-fat Milk:

Milk is an important source of calcium. And a glass of milk every day is very important to keep bones strong and body active. But the regular cow milk is enriched with fats, if you are drinking a glass of milk, it means along with calcium you are also taking in number of good and bad fats. So, try to shift from regular milk to low-fat milk.

Low-fat milk has all the good fats that the body needs plus a huge amount of calcium to keep you strong and healthy.

Whole Grains, Eggs, and Cereals:

Whole grains, eggs, and cereals are the best source of protein. Protein is important to keep you active even after a hectic day. Protein prevents the body against all the aging effects. It is better to say that proteins are the best anti-aging foods.

The best thing is to take raw proteins in your everyday meals. And the egg, cereals, and lentils are the best form of proteins that you can have in everyday meals.

Also, start your day with a simple cereal and an egg, it helps you to stay active and you won't feel lazy at all.

Drink A Lot Of water:

If you are taking all the healthy meals in a day but ignoring good intake of water, I am telling you, it is not good for your health at all. The human body has 97% water and it is very important to keep yourself hydrated.

Ideally, doctors suggest drinking 14 glasses of water every day.

Lentils:

Eating a lot of lentils in your everyday meal is the best way to keep yourself healthy. Lentils are enriched with proteins and other nutrients. The best way of taking lentils is to boil them in water for half an hour and make a soup with little spices and salt. Have a bowl of this soup daily or twice a week. Intake of a lot of lentils helps in reducing the risk of heart disease, some kinds of cancer and diabetes. Lentils are the best source of proteins especially for the people who are following healthy diet plans or trying to reduce weight quickly.

So, try to include lentils as part of your everyday meal and stay happy and healthy.

Fasting and Its Proven Health benefits

So by now, we have understood that fasting is a diet activity that means no food for certain time periods. It has a lot of proven health benefits. Let's have a look at them.

Control Blood Sugar:

A few examinations have discovered that fasting may improve glucose control, which could be particularly valuable for those in danger of diabetes. Truth be told, according to some recent research that includes 10 individuals with type 2 diabetes demonstrated that transient irregular fasting altogether diminished glucose levels in the blood and regulate the amount of insulin it. Moving on another audit found that both alternate-day fasting and 24 hours fasting was as successful as constraining calorie consumption at lessening insulin obstruction.

Diminishing insulin opposition can build your body's affectability to insulin, permitting it to move glucose from your circulation system to your cells all the more effectively. So, your body has a lower risk of diabetes and it has a more regulated amount of sugar in the blood. Combined with the potential glucose bringing down impacts of fasting, this could help keep your glucose consistent, forestalling spikes and crashes in your glucose levels.

Also, it is important to keep in mind that fasting has a different impact on different people.

For example, one little, three-week study indicated that practicing alternate-day fasting weakened glucose control in women however it does not affect men like that.

Precisely we can say that fasting is very useful to regulate blood sugar levels and to reduce the amount of insulin in the body. If you want to lead a diabetes-free life then one healthiest way is to start intermittent fasting right away.

Changes Functions of cells and Hormone:

When you do not eat for a long period of time, a lot of things happen to your body including cells repairing processing and certain other hormones activity. Not eating for a longer period of time burns unused calories and fats that help in weight reduction.

Following other changes occurs when you are fasting.

- The blood level of growth hormones increases by 5 times during fasting.

- There are certain changes in genes and molecules that prevent the body against many diseases.

- The process of cell repairing becomes faster.

Fights Inflammations:

Though inflammation has a lot of health benefits, it prevents the body against certain disease but at the same time, acute inflammation can lead to serious health consequences. According to some research done, chronic inflammation can lead the human body towards dangerous diseases including heart disease, some types of cancer and arthritis. Fasting helps the human body to fight against chronic inflammation. A study was conducted having 15 adults fasting for a few days, resulting in having fewer levels of body inflammation.

So in short, we can say that fasting helps in the reduction of inflammation thus provokes a healthy lifestyle.

Belly Fat Reduction:

A large number of individuals who are doing intermittent fasting is getting more fit, of course, the healthy lifestyle is only the purpose of fasting. (I am going to discuss fasting and weight loss in detail below) As a rule, irregular fasting will cause you to eat fewer suppers.

Except if on the off chance that you repay by eating substantially more during different dinners, you will end up having a lesser amount of calories in your belly. At times when you are fasting, all the extra fats and calories are being burned. And that results in belly reduction. Moreover, irregular fasting upgrades hormone capacity to encourage weight reduction.

Lower insulin levels, higher development hormone levels and expanded measures of norepinephrine (noradrenaline) all expand the breakdown of muscle to fat ratio and encourage its utilization for vitality.

So precisely we can say that fasting really builds your metabolic rate by 3.6-14% and helps in belly reduction. At the end of the day, intermittent fasting chips away at the two sides of the calorie condition. It supports your metabolic rate (builds calories out) and lessens the measure of nourishment you eat.

According to researchers conducted back in 2014 analytics shows that intermittent fasting can cause weight reduction of 3-8% more than 3-24 weeks (12). People practicing intermittent fasting initially lost 4-7% of their extra weight which demonstrates that they lost heaps of tummy fat, the destructive fat in the stomach hole that causes infections and many other hazardous diseases including obesity and heart diseases.

In other surveys conducted on intermittent fasting, it has been reported that fasting caused less muscle misfortune and helps in calorie management.

Taking everything into account, I can briefly say that fasting can be a fantastically incredible weight reduction instrument.

Improved Heart Health:

A healthy body must have a healthy heart. According to a survey, heart diseases are one of the major causes of death around the globe. Heart attacks due to thinning of veins and arteries, high cholesterol levels in the blood are the few major heart diseases. Fasting helps a lot in making your heart strong and healthy. Healthy fasting hours contributes a lot in heart health and helps your heart to perform in better ways. One survey showed that two months of alternate-day fasting decreased degrees of "terrible" LDL cholesterol and blood triglycerides by 25% and 32% individually. It means fasting is highly helpful in reducing the bad cholesterol level in blood. And purifies the blood as well.

One more research conducted on 100 adults has indicated that fasting for three weeks under clinical supervision altogether diminished circulatory strain, just as levels of blood triglycerides, all-out cholesterol, and "terrible" LDL cholesterol. So instead of taking heavy drugs that are heavy on both "body" and "pocket", it is better to try the intermittent fasting and keep your body healthy and active.

Intermittent fasting is also beneficial in other diseases just as an altogether lower danger of diabetes, which is a significant hazard factor for coronary illness.

In short, it is wise to say that fasting is helpful in maintaining heart health and to avoid many heart-related diseases including heart attack. According to an estimate, 31.5% across the world die every year because of heart diseases. And the simplest and easiest solution to cure all these diseases is nothing but just intermittent fasting.

Boost Brain Cells and Nervous system:

Not only body but fasting has a lot of healthy impact on brain cells and its activities as well. According to research that is mainly conducted on animals it has been seen that fasting helps in recovering brain cells and to give a better nervous system to the body. Intermittent fasting for 11 months or more can improve both brain cells and brain structure. Fasting also helps in better cognitive systems by producing more nerve cells.

As I have mentioned earlier that fasting helps the body to fight against inflammation, it could thus also be helpful in fighting against many neurodegenerative disorders and other diseases like Alzheimer's and Parkinson's.

Though this research has been conducted on animal brains, there is a lot more to come about the human brain as well. Precisely we can say that fasting helps in boosting brain cells and brain structure.

Better Growth Hormone Secretion:

The human development hormone is a kind of protein hormone that is vital to numerous parts of your body. It helps in the growth and development of various body parts and keeps the body active and strong. According to some researchers conducted on the human body, it has been shown that this key hormone is associated with development, digestion, weight reduction and muscle quality. A few investigations have discovered that fasting could normally build HGH levels and stimulates its secretion in the body thus resulting in better growth and development process.

Research conducted on 10 adults indicated that fasting for 24 hours essentially expanded degrees of human development harmony. Another little examination in 9 adults found that fasting for only two days prompted a 5-overlay increment in the HGH creation rate.

Furthermore, fasting may help keep up consistent glucose and insulin levels for the duration of the day, when the human body is intake no foods and solids which may additionally upgrade levels of HGH as some exploration has discovered that continuing expanded degrees of insulin may diminish HGH levels. So precisely we can say that fasting helps a lot in muscle and body growth because it stimulates the activity of human development and growth hormones.

Long Life Span:

There is nothing wrong with saying that fasting helps to reduce the aging effects. Hence ensuring a longer and healthier life span. Many types of research have been conducted on animal bodies that show fasting can result in a longer life span and decrease all the aging effects. It includes aged diseases and a lot of other problems as fasting helps in the process of blood purification, it makes skin glow differently. Fasting is like a filter that filter away all the negative and harmful effects from your body. Only leaving back the healthiest nutrients, hormones and body cells.

One other research that was conducted on rats shows that the rats who were fasting for a few consecutive days have a better and healthier life span as compared to the one who did not. The fasting rats have an 83% better life span. Other than rats, the research has been conducted on some other animals as well. They also resulted in the same manner. Though these studies have been only conducted on animal bodies yet. Scientists and health experts believe that they work similarly on the human body as well.

Prevents various Kind of Cancers:

According to some researchers conducted on animals and test tubes, it has been proved that fasting helps in prevention and fighting various kinds of cancerous cells. Actually, one rodent study found that other day fasting helped square tumor arrangement.

Correspondingly, a test-tube study indicated that presenting malignancy cells to a few patterns of fasting was as compelling as chemotherapy in deferring tumor development and expanded the viability of chemotherapy. In other words, we can say that fasting helps chemotherapy to make the body fight against cancerous cells.

Most researches conducted are on animals mostly but it is believed that they have some results on the human body as well. There is still a lot more to come about the human body and fasting. Now we all are looking forward to extra investigations. It is expected to see how fasting may impact malignant growth advancement and treatment in people.

Helps in better Sleep:

Have you ever felt that after having a big feast you feel sleepy immediately? It means your food has a direct impact on your sleep as well.

According to some research, it is stated that fasting has a direct impact on your sleep patterns and it helps to give you better sleep at night. It is stated that a person who is fasting for several weeks would fall asleep quickly and he will wake up fresher and more active. It is suggested that a human should take his last meal a few hours before sleeping. Because the digestion process works best when you are awake and active. Once you lay down in your bed, the digestion becomes slower. Sleeping with a heavy stomach disturbs sleep patterns and might result in nightmares and other irritations including heavy acid reflux, and heartburn, which makes sleep harder.

Side Effects of Intermittent Fasting:

People who love intermittent fasting often ignore the fact that intermittent dieting is not for everyone. It might have some side effects if you are not doing it right. Also, intermittent fasting does not benefit everyone. You can also mix up intermittent fasting with some other diet plans like Keto diet. We are going to discuss Keto Vs intermittent diet in detail. It is very important to figure out which intermittent diet method suits your body. Every method is not for everybody. The human body has different levels of hunger resistance and hormone production. Everybody's reaction to intermittent fasting is different.

Though we can't ignore the fact that intermittent fasting has a lot of health benefits. The above mentioned are just a few of them. There are a lot more advantages that are great for the human body and increase the lifespan of humans as well. But on the other hand, there are also some negative impacts of intermittent fasting. Anyone who is going to start intermittent fasting anytime soon needs to know both the positive and negative impacts of intermittent fasting and then decide either its beneficial for your body or not.

So, let's read out what are possible side effects of intermittent fasting on the human body.

Fatigue:

The human body needs a lot of energy to work properly. Every task we are doing needs a certain amount of energy and this energy comes from the food we eat. Even when we are sleeping, our body continues to work and the body metabolism is still there. It means the human body is in a state of work 24/7 and it needs energy every time. Once you start fasting for a longer period of time like 8-10 hours, you start feeling fatigued and brain fog. It feels like you are tired all the time and not ready to work. Fasting requires a lot of motivation and hard work. If you are thinking eating no food for hours and hours is just a simple task then you might be very wrong.

Even skipping a single meal sometimes leads you toward laziness and dizziness. There are times in fasting when you make certain blunders even without thinking, you feel like your mind is just absent and you do not have the power to think of any new thought. This situation is because of fatigue and brain fog. If something like this is happening to you, it means you need to fast for shorter periods of time and eat more healthy food at times when you are not fasting. Changing the fasting method might also help. The fasting and health experts say that "you can eat whatever you want to eat during intermittent fasting, but always keep in mind the purpose of intermittent fasting" that is why it is important to eat healthy meals in non-fasting hours to keep your body more active and strong.

Feeling Hungry Most of the Time:

The human body has an addiction to food and no one can survive without it and that is a fact. Even just skipping a meal makes you hungry and lazy. I do not know if I am using the right word or not but hunger is one of the biggest side effects of fasting. A person who has just started fasting might feel hungry all the time. There is a continuous feeling of grumpiness and irritation that tells your mind that you are hungry. Fasting needs a lot of patience and you need to tell your body how it is done in a proper manner.

There is a pro tip to avoid this laziness and tiredness feeling in the morning. That is to take a lot of protein a few hours before fasting. Proteins give your body the energy that helps you to sustain your fast in a better way. The protein foods are eggs, meat, fish, lentils and it is better to eat raw fruits and vegetables to get your energy back.

Food Obsessions:

Being on any sort of prohibitive eating or any kind of diet plan or fasting can influence your relationship with food, says a very famous health expert Koen's. While a few people like the inflexibility of intermittent fasting, others may wind up concentrating an excess amount of food when they can eat and what number of calories they are getting.

Investing an exorbitant measure of energy considering the quality or amount of your nourishment consistently can prompt a kind of dietary problem called orthorexia. As indicated by The National Eating Disorders Association, having orthorexia means you might discover food obsessions. You might be thinking about food all the time when you can't have it. The only thought that you can ever think of while fasting is to break the fast.

That should not be the objective of any eating routine, says Koen's: "You need to concentrate on framing a sound, positive relationship with nourishment."

Hair Loss:

You might not believe that but fasting for longer periods and not taking enough nutrients and vitamins may result in chronic hair loss. Human hair needs a lot of vitamins and zinc. The deficiency of vitamin D and zinc might be one of the causes of hair loss. If you see that more hair is falling off during your shower it means your body needs of nutrition are not fulfilled properly and you need to stop fasting right now. Or one other way is to start taking multivitamin supplements.

Especially the people who are doing intermittent fasting for weight loss, they might lose many body nutrition and fats that would cause hair loss and some other serious issues as well that need to get addressed in time. Consult your doctor or any other health expert as soon as possible in any severe case of hair loss.

Low Blood sugar:

In case you are continually feeling dizziness, nausea, headache, or fatigue during the fasting hours, it means your body is throwing up. And the sugar level in blood is getting lower. That is the time to stop fasting right away or to get yourself checked properly from your doctor. It might reduce the insulin level in the blood to the point that it becomes dangerous for the body. It is stated in many reports that excessive fasting might be dangerous for people who are suffering from type 2 diabetes.

If you are diabetic and want to start intermittent fasting, then it is very important to select the right method for it. Otherwise, your body might just throw up and you might collapse at any time of day. It is recommended to take some low fat and less sugary juices during fasting hours to keep blood sugar level to normal. Or you can simply add half a spoon of brown sugar in water with a pinch of salt and drink it once a day. It gives the body a certain amount of sugar and helps you to sustain the fast without body collapse.

Change in the Menstrual Cycle:

Here is another side effect of intermittent fasting. You might feel a change in your menstrual cycle. It happens when a woman loses a huge amount of weight at once and does not get the proper calories and nutrition. It might result in changed or disturbed period cycles. According to some research's women with very smart weak bodies suffer from a situation that is commonly known as "Amenorrhea " that is a disease in which either period slows down or they get completely stopped. If any of you are going through this situation because of intermittent fasting, I suggest you stop right away and consult your gynecologist. There is nothing more important than your health. As I said it before too "health is wealth"

Sudden weight loss might disturb your hormones and genes. It might result in other period-related problems like facial hair growth or body pains especially backaches and leg pain. All of these things happen because of nothing but weakness and an insufficient number of vitamins, nutrition, and proteins in the body. That is why it is suggested that people who are on their intermittent fasting, especially talking about women, must take some multivitamins supplements to ignore all these health-related issues.

Sleep Disturbance:

Here I am not denying the fact that fasting helps a person to fall asleep quickly. As we have discussed it already. It is because it helps you fight against late-night snack habits and when you lay down on the bed, the digestion process is done already. And a person can sleep in peace without any heartburn or acid reflux. But according to some research, the effect of fasting on all humans is not the same. Different sleeping patterns have been observed in different human beings depending upon their body capabilities and nature.

In research conducted in 2018, it has been stated that fasting might disturb your sleep patterns if your body is running low on nutrition and vitamins. It is also said that fasting during day time might affect the human "rapid Eye Movement " and can lead to other different problems including cognitive processing, loss of memory and concentration.

Again, if you have started intermittent fasting and facing any irritation or disturbance in your sleep patterns, then it is the right time to give a pause and consult some health experts. Talk about all the problems that might be disturbing your sleep patterns and get the pre medication done. Again, just for your reminder, if your body is not capable of intermittent fasting, you can stop it right away. There are many other useful diet plans like Keto that might help you in healthy weight loss. So, consult your doctor and decide which diet plan suits your body the best.

Constipation:

Yes, you read it right. If you are going through slow bowel movement or not getting any at all, it might be because of intermittent fasting. It indicates that your body is running low on fibers and fluids. That is why all health experts always suggest drinking lots of water or other fluids during fasting hours. And to take raw vegetables and fruits, fruits and vegetables are enriched sources of fiber. And fiber helps in bowel movement.

If you are going through any bowel movement problem or not getting any bowel in 24hours, I would suggest you start drinking a lot of water. It will prevent you from dehydration as well as from constipation. But in case it gets severe and the problem is not being solved from water as well, it is time to take a pause and consult some health experts.

Unhealthy meals:

Though there is not any chance of severe eating disorder as a result of intermittent fasting it might trigger some unhealthy eating habits. That is because, in a non-fasting hour, people just try to cover up to 5000-6000 calories to get back all the energy. Even thinking about what they are eating and either it would help them in serving the purpose of intermittent fasting. All health experts suggest taking healthy meals that are enriched with proteins, fats, and fibers. Let's talk about what a healthy meal should consist of later on.

In 16 hours of intermittent fasting, a person feels so hungry that he/she can end up eating everything that is present in their fridge or on the kitchen table. Hunger does not let people concentrate on what they are taking in. That is why before starting intermittent fasting it is important to set a goal for a healthy meal every time you break your fast.

Mood Changes:

Whatever you eat has a direct impact on your mood. I have been listening to this statement for a long period of time and now I have realized how food has a direct impact on human mood swings. When you are fasting, you might notice some severe mood changes like irritation, severe anger, or a great boost of energy or motivation once you get used to fasting and many others. Few people become so aggressive and impatient that they might lose their job or any other important activity. The mood swings are so adverse at times that you can't resist emotions like crying, shouting and sometimes hitting someone hard. These mood changes are chronic and it indicates that something very wrong is going on in your body. If this happens to you or any of your friends, I advise you to stop intermittent fasting at that very moment. Take a long breath and then consult any good doctor.

Most of the time, people do not consider mood swings as a severe side effect of intermittent fasting. But this concept is wrong. Your mood has a direct impact on your brain and body health. The happiest person looks healthy and strong as compared to a sad or a confused person. I would suggest you always select a diet plan that does not affect your mood that much.

These are all the reported side effects of intermittent fasting. In case you have been following intermittent fasting for a longer period of time, and see no side effects, then it is okay to continue. But in case any of the above negative impacts have been seen in your body, stop fasting and decide some other diet plan for yourself.

Below is a brief detail of what a healthy meal should consist of, and what the meaning of healthy eating is.

A Healthy Diet Plan for Non-Fasting Hours:

The Concept of a healthy diet has been wronged for many years. It is assumed that being healthy means eating less and staying ultra-thin which is not true at all. A healthy diet means the intake of foods that keeps your mind and body active, reduces fats and has a positive impact on your mood as well.

A healthy diet plan is to set the proper proportion of fats, proteins, calcium, and carbohydrates with lots of water.

The following ingredients are the fundamentals of a healthy meal plan.

Fiber:

Do not forget to add fiber to your daily meals. Fiber enriched foods like vegetables, fruits, grains and nuts should be part of your healthy diet plan. Fiber has a lot of benefits but the most important one is, it prevents your body against heart disease, strokes, and heart attack. It is important for the purification of blood and prevents constipation. Fiber is also important for healthy and glowing skin.

Calcium:

While preparing a healthy diet plan, do not forget to add Calcium to it. Calcium is very important to keep your bones strong. The deficiency of calcium leads to lazy and unhealthy bones. Also, less consumption of calcium can lead you towards osteoporosis, depression, and anxiety. A glass of milk along with calcium-enriched foods like coconut, cheese, Mozzarella, yogurt, cream, and cereals should be part of your everyday diet.

Protein:

Proteins should be a part of your healthy diet plan. As we age, our body requires more intake of proteins to keep us going. Proteins are essential for keeping our body and mind fresh and help us to perform daily chores properly.

The people suffering from protein deficiency might face some health problems like pain in bones and laziness. On the other hand, intake of too many protein supplements like tablets etc. is dangerous for kidneys.

The best way to intake protein is through healthy food like meat, fresh vegetables and a boiled egg for breakfast. Try to consume a proper portion of protein every day to keep yourself active and strong.

Carbohydrates:

Carbohydrates are known as carbohydrates because they consist of carbon, hydrogen, and oxygen. Carbohydrates are sugary elements found in most of the foods. They are starch basically that help in the control of sugar level and body insulins. Carbohydrates are mostly present in all fruits and vegetables, in rice and wheat. Every food that leaves a sweet taste on your tongue after you have chewed it, indicates that it is carbohydrate enriched food.

Precisely we can say that it is a big source of energy for your body. Carbohydrates in proper proportions are important to keep you active and strong. Try taking foods that have plenty of carbohydrates like wheat, cereals, dry fruits, fruits, and all other vegetables. It is better to take carbohydrates in their natural form instead of supplements that are being sold in the market.

Fats:

Our body consists of two kinds of fats. Good fats and bad fats. Good fats are those who help in keeping the body strong and active. Good fats come from foods like butter, chicken, fish, meat, and vegetables. It is important to take the proper intake of good fats in everyday meals when you are not fasting. On the other hand, bad fats are those who are being burned when you are fasting for a long period of time. These fats include belly fats that can result in many chronic diseases if they stay in the body for a longer period of time. Bad fats might result in heart diseases. Cholesterol or increased sugar level in blood.

Myths About intermittent fasting

Though intermittent fasting has become so famous in the last few years. I believe every health-conscious person knows about intermittent fasting, its types, and benefits. But everything you hear about it is not true at all. Many people to associate some kinds of myths with intermittent fasting and these are not so true.

Below are some myths related to intermittent fasting and frequency foods that you should not believe. Let's find out what they are.

Intermittent fasting leads you towards Starving mode:

It is a very popular argument against intermittent fasting is that it places your body into starvation mode, hence closing down your digestion and keeping you from gaining a lot of fats and calories. While the facts confirm that long haul weight reduction can diminish the number of calories you consume after some time, this happens regardless of what weight reduction technique you use. If it is intermittent fasting, Keto diet plan or any other diet plan prescribed by your doctor.

The truth is that there is no proof that irregular fasting causes a more noticeable decrease in calories consumed than other weight reduction techniques. We can say that fasting for a longer period of time may expand your metabolic rate. This is because of an extreme increase in blood levels of norepinephrine, which invigorates your digestion and educates your fat cells to the separate muscle to fat ratio. Studies uncover that fasting for as long as 48 hours can help digestion by 3.6–14%. But in case if you are fasting more than that then the impacts can switch, diminishing your digestion.

Precisely, this myth related to intermittent fasting is not true at all. So, there is no need to overthink this false rumor and you can continue to your intermittent fasting method without worrying about it. Also, do not forget to eat healthy meals when you are breaking your fast. As meals also stimulate hunger and healthy meals are digested more easily.

Skipping breakfast makes you fat:

There is one very famous myth related to breakfast. It is said that skipping breakfast might lead to excessive hunger, food cravings and huge amounts of weight loss. We grew up listening to this myth that breakfast is the most important meal of the day and skipping it might cause many health problems including dizziness and lazy day ahead. A 16 weeks study was conducted that involves more than 200 adults shows that there is no apparent sign of weight gain in the people who skip their breakfast as compared to one who has had healthy breakfast for all these weeks.

There is no doubt in the fact that different human bodies have different reactions to certain meal skipping. There might be a possibility of weight gain but these cases are not very prominent. All the diet plans including Keto includes a healthy breakfast and it helps in weight reduction as well. But in case you are practicing intermittent fasting and the method is 24 hours fasting from breakfast-breakfast then relax it is okay to continue this method of fasting.

I am not denying the fact that eating breakfast keeps you more active at your job or in schools. Having a healthy breakfast with lots of proteins and milk is a healthy habit and everyone should have this healthy eating habit but I am just denying this myth that skipping breakfast makes you fat.

Precisely we can say that breakfast is a healthy habit for maximum people but you can also skip it without having any bad consequences on your health.

Eating frequency results in better Metabolism:

There is another myth related to frequently eating. Many people believe that eating frequent meals after every few hours improves the metabolism of the body and helps to burn more calories. For your information, this myth is not true at all. There is a process named "thermic effect" of the body that helps in burning calories. According to some studies and health experts, this thermic effect expands some calories while digesting food. According to an estimate thermic effects use 10% of your total calories' intake. So, it does not matter if you are taking 6 meals a day or 3 meals a day. The total amount of burned calories while metabolism remain10 percent of the total calorie intake.

The fact is that the total number of calories that you are taking in matters only but not how many meals you are having per day. Studies have confirmed that an increase or decrease of meal frequency does not have any impact on the number of calories burned and the metabolism rate of the body. So, this Myth has been proved wrong and there is no truth in it.

All that matters is eating healthy either it is into heavy meals or in 4 small meals.

Brain functions better with regular supply glucose:

Some people who are against intermittent fasting and have no faith in its benefits and contribution towards weight loss believe that frequent meals are better than fasting for long hours. It is a myth that frequent meals provide a regular supply of glucose to the brain and helps it to function in more proper manners. On the other hand, long hours of fasting may affect brain cells and its activity. This myth is not true at all.

A few people guarantee that in case you do not eat carbs like clockwork, your mind will quit working. It is believed that carbs are enriched in glucose and they are best for brain cells growth and its activity. This depends on the conviction that your cerebrum can just utilize glucose for fuel. In any event, during long haul fasting, starvation, or extremely low-carb slims down, your body can create ketone bodies from dietary fats Ketone bodies can take care of parts of your mind, lessening its glucose necessity fundamentally.

A few people report feeling exhausted or temperamental when they do not eat for some time. In the event that this concerns you, you ought to think about keeping snacks available or eating all the more much of the time. As we have discussed earlier as well that eating healthy during non-fasting hours helps to make both body and brain strong. If you are having a proper diet while non-fasting hours, fasting for 8-10 hours won't disturb your mind or any of its activity.

Frequent eating helps in quick weight loss:

Weight loss is a long journey that involves a lot of effort and hard works. Many people have different beliefs and myths related to weight loss procedure. Some think intermittent fasting helps and others are denying its benefits and impacts.

Critics of intermittent fasting believe that fasting is a long-term weight loss process and it takes a lot of effort as well as a lot of time. Instead of fasting for a longer time period it is better to have frequent meals every 5-6 hours. Frequent meals help in quick weight loss. So, for all those who think that this myth is correct, note down that there Is no reality in this myth.

Since frequent meals do not have any positive or negative impact on your body's metabolism, likewise it does not have any impact on your weight loss process. A study was conducted involving 16-17 adults and it has been noticed that the number of meals intake does not have any difference in weight loss, fat loss, or loss of appetite. Some people also have a point of view that fasting for longer hours provokes fast-breaking with heavy feasts thus affecting all the healthy eating habits. So, if you are the one who thinks the same, and wants to intake fewer calories while having frequent meals per day, stick to it. Every person has a different body and it has a different reaction to several diet plans. Find the one that is more effective for your body and that helps you in quick weight loss.

Precisely there is no evidence that changing your meal habits can have any impact on your weight loss journey.

Frequent eating has many health benefits:

Some people believe in the Myth that eating frequent meals has certain health benefits but just as frequent eating does not have any impact on weight loss or metabolic rate of the body, the same is the case with this myth as well. Frequent eating does not have any apparent health benefits. On the contrary intermittent fasting has more health benefits and it prevents the body against many chronic diseases as we have discussed it earlier. In addition to that intermittent fasting also involves a process called autophagy, in which your body cells utilize old and broken proteins for vitality. These proteins are stored in your body for longer periods of time. And as you eat frequently the body fails to consume old proteins, as the new proteins keep coming in. also, there is no doubt in the fact Autophagy may help secure against maturing, malignant growth, and conditions like Alzheimer's infection.

Along these lines, intermittent fasting has different advantages for your body metabolism. We have discussed that in detail already. A few investigations even recommend that nibbling or eating all the time hurts your wellbeing and raises your danger of sickness. For instance, one investigation found that an unhealthy eating routine with various suppers caused a considerable increase in liver fat, showing a higher danger of greasy liver illness. That is fatal for human health. Furthermore, some other studies conducted on few adults show that individuals who eat all the more frequently have a lot higher danger of colorectal cancer.

Intermittent fasting makes you lose muscles:

There is a misconception that when you fast, your body starts burning all the proteins as well as muscle mass. That results in losing muscle mass quickly and you look old and weak. This intermittent fasting related myth is not true at all. Although this happens when you follow a diet plan without deciding any healthy meals and instead of fasting for a few hours, you believe in starving. Intermittent fasting has no such proven side effects. In fact, in different studies conducted, it has stated that intermittent fasting is helpful in weight loss without any loss of muscle mass.

There are many intermittent fasting methods that rather help in the increase of muscular mass. In one review it is written that intermittent fasting results in quick weight loss with no or zero reduction of muscle mass as compared to other dieting procedures. In addition to that many health, experts confirmed that fasting helps in gaining muscle mass instead of its reduction. Many bodybuilders and frequent gym-going people confirm that fasting helps them in gaining more muscle mass. So, in short, we can conclude that this myth is wrong and there's no evidence that fasting causes more muscle loss than conventional calorie restriction.

Intermittent Fasting provokes the habit of overeating:

A few people guarantee that irregular fasting makes you indulge in a huge amount of unhealthy meals during eating time windows. For all those who are practicing intermittent fasting or planning to do so, do not hear this myth at all because it is not true at all. The main purpose of intermittent fasting is to avoid all the heavy feasts and unhealthy diet plans. And to follow healthy diet meals in then on fasting hours. Developing overeating habits will definitely kill the purpose of intermittent fasting.

The facts confirmed that you lose a huge number of calories during fasting hours and gain a certain number of calories after breaking the fast. The amount that is required for a healthy body and brain. One investigation demonstrated that individuals who fasted for 24 hours just wound up eating around 500 additional calories the following day. This calorie count is far less than the 2,400 calories they'd missed during the fast. See how this myth has been proven wrong.

Since it reduces a large number of calories and regulates insulin levels while boosting digestion and norepinephrine levels, and human development hormone (HGH) levels, intermittent fasting causes you to lose fat.

Gaining fats because of intermittent fasting has no truth (everybody behaves differently to intermittent fasting but researches have shown it does not develop any overeating habits).

As indicated by one research, it is stated that fasting for 3–24 weeks caused normal weight and paunch fat misfortunes of 3–8% and 4–7%, individually. In other words, it is safe to say that intermittent fasting might be one of the most useful assets to get smarter and healthier.

Your body consumes a certain amount of protein per meal:

Some fitness freaks and critics of intermittent fasting believe that the human body consumes 30 grams of proteins per meal. It indicates that you should take more proteins after every 3-4 hours to maintain your muscle mass. However, this myth is not supported by any research or any other health expert. According to different research conducted shows that eating more doses of proteins does not have any impact on muscle loss or weight loss. The most important factor rather is the total amount of protein that you are taking in instead of taking small doses every 3-4 hours. In short, it is safe to say that this myth does not have any truth in it and your body can easily make use of more than 30 grams of protein per meal. It is unnecessary to obtain protein every 2–3 hours.

How to begin intermittent fasting:

By now, you must have understood that intermittent fasting is far different from other diet plans. Intermittent fasting does not focus on limiting the calories count but it is about not eating for several hours and let the old calories burn completely. Though intermittent fasting has a lot of health benefits it is not for everyone. As I have discussed earlier, before doing intermittent fasting you need to know about yourself, your body patience, its requirements, and all other important things. So, let's talk about how to start intermittent fasting. What steps should we need to follow before fasting?

Identify Goals:

Doing anything without setting a personal goal is of no use. No matter if it is a diet plan, exercise, walk or gym, you need to set a personal goal and then you work hard to achieve it. Setting a goal motivates you every day, and every new morning you wake up with an ambition to get that goal. The people who are planning to start intermittent fasting. I suggest them to write the personal goal once they have identified it on a paper and keep it on your study table. So, you see it every day and get motivated.

Your personal goal could be

- Weight loss.
- Muscle mass increase.
- Staying active and healthy.
- To avoid different diseases.
- To make your heart healthy and strong.
- To improve your patience.
- To check yourself, what you are capable of.
- To control sugar level in blood and regulate insulin and etc. etc.

Select the one from above and start working on it. Once you have selected the personal goal, now is the time to select the intermittent fasting method.

Select the Method:

Selecting a method of intermittent fasting is crucial yet a very important step. You need to identify your body capabilities first and then pick up the method that suits you the best. There are several intermittent fasting methods that we have already discussed in detail.

- 16:8 hours intermittent fasting.
- Warrior diet.
- Alternate day fasting.
- Eat stop eat
- 5:2 intermittent fasting method.

Once you have selected the intermittent fasting method, I would suggest you get stuck to it. Changing fasting methods after every several weeks does not have a good impact on your body health. Stick to one for months and find out if this method is useful to get the identified personal goal? Any person who has some medical issues like any heart disease, or types 2 diabetes must concern his doctor before starting any of the above-mentioned methods.

While deciding the fasting method one thing should be kept in mind that intermittent fasting and its methods are not about limiting the calorie count per meal. Instead of eating a window you can eat all the healthy foods and dishes that you liked the most. It is just about eating no food for hours.

But of course, if a person is doing it weight loss or muscle gain then you must select healthy diet plans full of nutrition, vitamins, fibers, fat, proteins, carbohydrates, and calcium. Eating unhealthy food might make it difficult for you to achieve your goal at the right time.

Find out caloric needs of the body:

Though there is no strict calories limitation when you are fasting but that does not mean calories do not count at all. If your body needs 5000 calories per day and you are having 8000 after breaking the fast then what is the actual use of fasting? Nothing. It means you are just wasting it. Once your goal is identified, now you can find out the caloric needs of your body. If the person is doing intermittent fasting for weight loss, then, of course, he needs to eat fewer calories than usual.

But in case the purpose of fasting is to gain muscle mass or weight then the calorie intake would be more than usual. Well, there are many tools available that help a person to identify are caloric needs of his body. If you fail to identify it yourself you can always visit your doctor or health care expert to help you out in this regard.

Pick up a meal plan:

Once you have identified your goal and the method of intermittent fasting, now it is easy for you to make a meal plan for yourself. It is time to decide how many calories you are going to take in while fasting and in non-fasting hours. According to some health experts, it is okay to have 500-600 calories while you are fasting. 500 calories are ideal for women whereas 600 calories suit best to the requirement of man's body. In intermittent fasting, we are not very strict about calorie intake but we just make sure we are eating healthy and fulfilling all the nutritional needs of the body. Meal planning offers many benefits, including helping a person stick to their calorie count. In addition to that meal plans also make sure that the person has all the necessary food on hand for cooking recipes, quick meals, and snacks, etc.

So, either you are doing intermittent fasting for weight loss, or for muscle gain, it is important to have a healthy meal plan by your side to follow it regularly.

Fasting goes back to antiquated people who regularly went hours or days between dinners as getting nourishment. It was a trouble back then because people didn't have much knowledge about diet plans and healthy meals. The human body adjusted to this style of eating, permitting stretched out periods to follow healthy eating and healthy style.

Intermittent fasting has now replaced the old methods of fasting and now we can see much newer in it. At the point when an individual attempt an irregular fast for dietary proposes, it tends to be exceptionally viable for weight reduction. Indeed, as indicated by one examination, a great many people attempt fasting to help shed pounds.

Other research backs up the cases that fasting can enable an individual to get in shape. For instance, a survey of studies shows that numerous individuals who quickly observe a higher loss of instinctive muscle versus fat and alike somewhat less decrease in body weight contrasted and individuals who follow progressively customary calorie decrease eat fewer carbs.

Intermittent fasting for weight loss: All you need to know:

As we have already discussed a lot of things related to intermittent fasting, its types, methods, benefits, side effects, how to start it and all the myths related to intermittent fasting. Now is the time to share the people's weight loss journeys, their success story and all other things that you must need to know about intermittent fasting and weight loss. According to Los Angeles Times, intermittent fasting has become a new fashion to lose 100 pounds and people are sharing their successful weight loss stories.

Cynthia Bella, a 40 years old police detective and mother of two tell here successful weight loss stories. She said "skipping breakfast would make her feel so fantastic" she never thought about it in her life. Talking about her intermittent fasting method Bella told that she eats from 11 am to 8 pm window and fast for the rest of 15 hours. Bella has tried so many other weight loss diet plans but she failed to get the desired results every time. Intermittent fasting is the only way out for her and in just a few months she already lost 15 pounds and 4 inches of her waist. Bella reported that 15 hours of fasting keeps her fresh and active at her job and at home too. In the eating window, she eats healthy meals and takes a lot of nutrition and vitamins. Eating her dinner at 8 pm helps her to get better sleep at nice without any heartburn and acid reflux.

Colleen Tylor, a 52-year-old military wife shared her successful weight loss journey with the help of intermittent fasting. Collen started intermittent fasting with a shorter period and now she is fasting for 24 hours twice a week. Collin said she lost 100 pounds of her waist with the help of intermittent fasting and she is quite happy with all the results. Intermittent fasting has become somewhat of a darling in the wellness world. Results from many clinical investigations on intermittent fasting, investigating its effect on ailment just as symptoms, are relied upon to turn out in 2020.

Meanwhile, we conversed with fasting specialists to think of a rundown of eight things you should know before trying intermittent fasting for weight loss. let's read out what they are.

You do not have to bind yourself to "8 hours eating window":

Many health experts have confirmed that you do not need to bind yourself to eight hours eating window in intermittent fasting. You get the benefit out of this fasting otherwise as well. Many people have already assumed that intermittent fasting is about eight hours eating window only and it is a hard and fast rule of it if you want to lose weight to fight against some chronic disease, well this assumption is not true at all. You can still lose weight by switching the eating window to 10 and 12 hours as well. People who have more patience and tolerance towards food also fast for more than 16 to 18 hours and they are still getting their desired results. Research has shown that 10-12 hours eating window is as beneficial as 8 hours eating window. It also helps the body to lose belly fats, to fight against inflammation and regulate blood insulin level. So, if you also have this misconception, vanish that thought away. Fast according to your body strength and capability.

Every human body has a different tendency and patience.

A shorter Window is more beneficial:

The research that has been conducted last year at Alabama University has confirmed that a shorter eating window is however more beneficial as compared to the longer one. The research was conducted on two adults with an eating window of 6 hours and 12 hours. And the results show that the person with 6 hours eating window has more regulatory blood sugar and insulin level and he tends to lose weight more quickly. While it didn't essentially influence the quantity of calories members consumed, it lowered degrees of the hunger hormone ghrelin and expanded fat-consuming over the 24-hour day.

Intermittent fasting might not be a long-term weight loss strategy:

Though intermittent has been very useful when it comes to weight loss and a healthy body. But there is a risk of gaining weight as soon as you stop fasting. Your body gets addicted to the eating window and as soon as you stop fasting start eating 2-3 meals a day, there is a risk of gaining back all the weight you have shed. That is why it is important to maintain a healthy eating habit even if you have left intermittent fasting. Try eating raw fruits and vegetables and drink a lot of water to maintain the same body shape after leaving intermittent fasting.

The best tip is once you have got the desired body weight and now you want to skip intermittent fasting. Instead of leaving it at once, try to increase the time sap of the eating window. From 8 hours to 12 hours to 16 hours and then leave it slowly.

It is okay to have some cheat days:

Life is very unpredictable; you do not know what is coming in your way. There are a lot of unplanned things that might hit you by the way like a sudden friend wedding, or some fun vacation, dinner or lunch with colleagues' friends and family. In such kinds of events, it becomes difficult to follow one tight eating window. If you are a fitness freak and have no compromise on your health then there is nothing like that. But if you have no self-control when you see different kinds of food cuisines In Front on dinner table then it is okay to have a cheat day occasionally. On these kinds of occasions or events, you can follow 5;2

intermittent fasting methods. It means to eat normally for 5 days of the week and fast for two days. It will help you in enjoying your vacation without disturbing your weight loss efforts.

High Calories Beverages and drinks will break your fast:

One of the biggest problems with people practicing intermittent fasting is that they might break their fat accidentally without even knowing. Like adding an extra spoon of cream in your coffee or having high sugar beverages. Always remember that high calories beverages will break your fats. These beverages are high on calories and if you keep on consuming them, then there is no use of your intermittent fasting. Health experts and doctors advise people to take a lot of fluids during their fasting window but by fluids, they meant a lot of water and some coffee if you are addicted to it. Doctors recommend having at least 2-3 liters of water in the day. It keeps your body hydrated and does not stimulate hunger at once. Moreover, it gives you the strength to stay active while fasting.

"Eat Heavy breakfast and light dinner"

There is an old saying "eat breakfast like a king, supper like a prince and have dinner like a pauper" this is so true in case of intermittent fasting as well. Especially for the women who are striving for weight loss, it is better to have a heavy and healthy breakfast instead of breaking fast with a heavy feast. Many types of research have shown that the process of meal digestion is quicker in the daytime as compared to the night hours. So, if you had a heavy breakfast, the extra calories will burn out more quickly and will help you in your weight loss efforts.

It is not for everyone:

Always remember that intermittent fasting is not for everyone. If you have some medical problem it is better to get yourself a proper diet plan instead of starting intermittent fasting on your own. In addition to that Pregnant or breastfeeding women, or those who are underweight or have a history of eating disorders should not undertake a very strict intermittent fasting program, our experts said. Diabetics or anyone on medication should consult their doctor before starting any program.

Intermittent Fasting VS Keto: Should we combine these two?

Intermittent fasting and Keto diet are two of the hottest ways of reducing extra body weight right now. Millions of health-conscious people, or people suffering from obesity are following these two methods to shed some extra body pounds. Here the most commonly asked question by hundreds of people is

Is it safe to combine intermittent fasting with a keto diet? So, here Is the answer to this question as well as the potential benefits of combining both.

As of now, we have talked about intermittent fasting a lot. All of you are now well aware of everything related to intermittent fasting. On the other hand, the Keto diet is another very useful way of shedding bodyweight. Unlike intermittent fasting, keto is all about limiting calories and the intake of low carbs.

Carbs are regularly diminished to under 50 grams for each day, which powers your body to depend on fats rather than glucose for its primary vitality source In the metabolic procedure of human body that is commonly known as ketosis, your body separates fats to shape substances considered ketones that fill in as another fuel source This eating regimen is a successful method to shed pounds, yet it has a few different advantages also.

The keto diet has been utilized for almost a century to treat epilepsy and shows a guarantee for other neurological issues. Other than that, it has several other health benefits as well. For example, the keto diet may improve mental indications in individuals with Alzheimer's sickness Likewise, it might diminish the extra level of blood sugar and is very helpful for diabetic patients, improve insulin obstruction and lower coronary illness chance components like triglyceride levels.

Joining the ketogenic diet with intermittent fasting is likely safe for a great many people. Though both have separate health benefits, when you combine two of them, the number of health benefits will go on increasing. But to keep in mind pregnant or breastfeeding ladies and those who have some kind of eating disorder should not combine two of them without the doctor's advice. It is important to be concerned about health experts before combining keto with intermittent fasting. Also, Individuals with certain wellbeing conditions, for example, diabetes or coronary illness, ought to counsel with a specialist before giving discontinuous fasting a shot the keto diet.

Though keto and intermittent fasting have some proven benefits on human bodies according to studies and research, it does not have the same impact on everyone. The results might differ from person to person. A few people may find that fasting on the keto diet is excessively troublesome, or they may encounter unfriendly responses, for example, gorging on non-fasting days, fatigue and exhaustion Remember that Keep in mind that intermittent fasting is not necessary to reach ketosis. But we can say that it can be used as a tool to shed weight quickly. Basically, following a solid, balanced keto diet is sufficient for anybody hoping to improve wellbeing by eliminating carbs.

A Right Way to start Intermittent Fasting with Keto Diet:

The famous health care and doctors across the globe do not recommend you to start Keto and intermittent fasting both at the same time. If you are doing so it might be a big shock to your body from shifting to ketone instead of glucose as a fuel and at the same time fasting for longer hours. Research has shown staring both keto and fasting might result in the body collapse and also involves some other major health risks. That is why it is suggested by the health experts to start keto and follow it for 2-3 weeks. Once your body gets used to it, now you can start with intermittent fasting as well. One thing that should be kept in mind while combining both keto and fasting is to select the fasting hours wisely. It is best to start with 8 hours of fasting and then move on to 12 hours of fasting. Not more than that. 12 hours fasting from dinner to breakfast is the easy one, as most people do not eat late night snacks and this timing is a natural habit of theirs.

You can also shift your breakfasts and other suppers. Like, shift your breakfast to 11 am instead of 8 am. In case you want to increase your fasting timing. The only important thing that should be kept in mind is to avoid a sudden shift of any meal. Give your body a certain time to adjust with new changes otherwise this healthy combination would be of no use.

A Menu Guide for Intermittent fasting and Keto:

If you have decided to combine keto with intermittent fasting and got a green signal from your doctor as well. Now is the time to prepare a healthy meal menu for yourself. You must be thinking of what to eat as keto demands you to eat a few certain meals and intermittent fasting allows you to eat whatever you want. So, to your help herein a 3 days sample for the people who have just started keto fasting together.

Remember that the snacks in the given menu are just optional, moreover, there should be a proper proportion of carbs, fats, fibers, proteins, and vitamins. So, I would suggest you take a proper meal menu from your health expert and follow it strictly to get the desired results soon.

The following Menu is best if you are having 8 hours eating window along with keto.

DAY 1:

10 am (breakfast) scrambled eggs along with black coffee and avocados with lots of water.

1 pm (lunch) a large bowl of green leafy salad along with olive oil and grilled salmon fish.

3 pm (optional snacks): half a cup of nuts.

6 pm (dinner) chicken leg along with skin with a quarter cup of wild rice and 2 cups of Zucchini cooked in olive oil.

DAY 2:

10 a.m. Plain hot tea, one keto-friendly smoothie any flavor of your choice, with water.

1 p.m. Lunch 3 oz grilled chicken breast, half a plate filled with broccoli and 1 tablespoon of olive oil. And a full fresh avocado.

3 p.m. Snack (optional) coconut chips without sugar.

6 p.m. Dinner 3 oz seared tuna cooked in olive oil on a bed of Asian coleslaw, topped with a drizzle of olive oil and sesame seeds.

DAY 3:

10 a.m. Black coffee with keto chia pudding and water all morning

1 p.m. Lunch 3 egg omelet stuffed with peppers and spinach (1 cup) cooked in 1 tbsp olive oil.

Topped with half an avocado and sliced potatoes.

3 p.m. Snack (optional) Olives

6 p.m. large kale salad (3 cups) with 3 oz shrimp drizzled with 2 tbsp of olive oil and vinegar of your choice.

Potential Benefits of practicing both:

If you are following keto diet plans along with intermittent fasting then it has the following major potential benefits.

Smoothens Your Path to ketosis:

Intermittent fasting may enable your body to arrive at ketosis faster than the keto diet alone. That is because your body, when fasting, keeps up its vitality balance by moving its fuel source from carbs to fats the specific reason of the keto diet During fasting, insulin levels, and glycogen stores decline, driving your body to normally begin consuming fat for fuel. For any individual who battles to arrive at ketosis while on a keto diet, including intermittent fasting may successfully kick off your procedure.

May help you to lose more body fats:

Combining both Keto and intermittent fasting might help you to reduce your body fats more quickly as compared to keto alone. It is a fact that intermittent fasting has proven weight loss effects. As intermittent fasting for longer hours makes the metabolic rate of the human body more efficient and effective, it helps in burning fats that are stored in the body for too long. an 8-week study was conducted involving 14-16 individuals who rehearsed the 16/8 strategy of intermittent fasting. The results show that they lost almost 14% more muscle fat than those following an ordinary eating design. Thus, a survey of 28 investigations noticed that individuals who utilized irregular fasting lost a normal of 7.3 pounds (3.3 kg) more fat mass than those following extremely low-calorie counts calories.

In addition to that intermittent fasting may preserve muscle mass during weight reduction and improve vitality levels which might be useful for keto calorie counters hoping to improve athletic execution.

Side effects of combining Keto Diet with intermittent fasting:

World health organization has already stated the side effects of a keto diet. Keto might result in diarrhea, hair loss and nausea. Whereas we have already discussed the side effects of intermittent fasting already in detail. If not followed properly intermittent fasting might result in nausea, dizziness, laziness, hair loss, constipation and disturbed menstrual cycles in women. So, what happens when you combine the two. Are you ready for the combined side effects of the keto diet and intermittent fasting? So yes, according to some researches if you are not having proper nutrition and following diets properly that might result in severe side effects combining side effects of both keto and intermittent fasting. The combination of Keto and intermittent fasting needs a high level of patience and motivation. It is not a cup of tea for everyone and though not easy at all as well. If you have decided to combine both of them then you need to be very keen and motivated throughout the time. A little negligence might lead you towards some serious health problems.

Both keto and intermittent fasting are two complete diet plans and typically very difficult to follow. Combining them might add some extra challenges that are not at all easy for all the individuals. That is why all the health experts suggest to get proper and healthy diet plans and do not start this combination of keto and intermittent fasting without involving your doctor. The combination of intermittent fasting along with keto diet may assist you with arriving at ketosis quicker than a keto diet alone. It might likewise bring about discomfort to you or might lead you toward severe illness. While this technique may do some incredible things for a few, it is not important to blend both, and a few people ought to maintain a strategic distance from this mix.

You're free to test and see whether a blend or one practice all alone works best for you. Yet, similarly as with any significant way of life change, it is prudent to address your medicinal assistant first.

Intermittent fasting for women:

Intermittent fasting has a lot of benefits to health. We have discussed all the possible health benefits of intermittent fasting already. But some research has shown that intermittent fasting affects women in different manners compared to men. It is reported that intermittent fasting is not as beneficial to women as it is for men. One investigation indicated that blood sugar control and insulin regulation become worse in ladies following three weeks of fasting, which was not the situation in men. Men's bodies have more tolerance and sustenance to fasting.

There are additionally numerous episodic accounts of ladies who have encountered changes to their menstrual cycles after the beginning of intermittent fasting. It is reported that in the start few weeks of intermittent fasting women might face situations of less or absolutely no periods. Health experts at this stage advise women to stop fasting right away and get some medical help or multivitamins. Such incidents happen because female bodies are incredibly delicate to calorie limitation.

After fasting for a few weeks and taking fewer calories or fasting for a long time or too often a little piece of the cerebrum called the nerve center is influenced. This can upset the emission of gonadotropin-discharging hormone (GnRH), a hormone that helps discharge two contraceptive hormones: luteinizing hormone (LH) and follicle animating hormone (FSH)

There are times while practicing intermittent fasting when women hormones miss out communication with ovaries and as a result, women might face problems like irregular or no periods, infertility, weak bones, and backaches and a lot more other problems. Even though there are no practically identical human investigations or studies that have demonstrated that 3–6 months of intermittent fasting caused a decrease in ovary size and unpredictable conceptive cycles in females. Consequently, ladies ought to think about a changed way to deal with fasting, for example, shorter fasting periods and less fasting days.

Health Benefits of Intermittent Fasting for Women

Intermittent fasting not only helps you to reduce your waistline but it also has some other benefits on women's health. The best types for women include daily 14–16 hour fasts, the 5:2 diet or modified alternate-day fasting. While intermittent fasting is beneficial for heart health, diabetes and weight loss, some evidence indicates it may have negative effects on reproduction and blood sugar levels in some women. It is being said that modified versions of intermittent fasting appear safe for most women and maybe a more suitable option than longer or stricter fasts.

The following are some of the very prominent health benefits of intermittent fasting on women. Let's read them out.

Weight loss:

It has been already discussed in detail that intermittent fasting is one of the best ways of weight loss both in men and women. Numerous studies and research have shown that the effect of intermittent fasting regarding weight-loss is almost the same on both genders. There are few differences and health care declare them negligible differences. It ought to be noticed that the long-term impacts of intermittent fasting on weight reduction for ladies stay to be seen.

Temporarily, fasting appears to help in weight reduction. In any case, the sum you lose will probably rely upon the number of calories you expend during non-fasting periods and to what extent you cling to a healthy lifestyle. Starting intermittent fasting helps you to eat less compared to a normal day's diet.

One examination found that youngsters ate 650 fewer calories for each day when their nourishment admission was limited to a 4-hour eating window. Another investigation in 24 other adults, including both men and women, looks at the effects of 36-hour quick on dietary patterns. Despite eating additional calories on the post-quick day, members dropped their complete calorie balance by 1,900 calories, which is surely a critical decrease in the intake of calories.

Precisely it is safe to say that if you are a woman looking to lose weight or improve your health, intermittent fasting is something to consider.

Heart Health:

A healthy heart means a healthy body, if your heart is pumping blood in a normal manner and doing all his job perfectly it means you are a healthy human being. Researches and studies have shown that heart diseases are one of the major causes of deaths all around the world. Deaths of both men and women. One of the biggest causes of heart attack is obesity. One study has including 16 men and women have shown that obesity and increased LDL levels in blood results in shrinking of veins and thus lead towards many heart diseases especially heart attack.

Women practicing intermittent fasting have lesser chances of any heart diseases. Intermittent fasting makes your heart strong and healthy. Obese women must switch to intermittent fasting as soon as possible. Further studies have shown that intermittent fasting if done properly, can lower down LDL levels by 25% that is a good sign for heart health. There is a lot more room for further studies and researches to understand the full impact of intermittent fasting on women's heart health.

Precisely intermittent fasting has many positive effects on women's heart and it keeps it safe, strong and healthy.

Diabetes:

Diabetes is one of the major leading diseases in women especially women suffering from obesity. The researches have shown that women practicing intermittent fasting lowers the risk of diabetes and is healthier and more active as compared to one who does not practice any kind of fasting or diet plan. One study has shown that women who are doing intermittent fasting for a few weeks have regular blood sugar levels and insulin reduction. Intermittent fasting is a natural way to control blood sugar, blood pressure, and insulin reduction. A study conducted with more than 100 overweight or obese women shows that six months of intermittent fasting reduced insulin levels by 29% and insulin resistance by 19%. These results are quite surprising.

As compared to man, intermittent fasting is not as beneficial for women in terms of blood sugar. Researches have shown that man practicing intermittent fasting have more controlled blood sugar level as compared to women. A small study has also shown that after 22 weeks of fasting, blood sugar levels for women can get worse but there are no such signs in man's body. But despite this, the reduction in insulin level prevents women's body against diabetes.

Best Type of intermittent fasting for women:

The researches have shown that women should select the intermittent fasting method that has a shorter fasting period. Especially in the beginning start with 8 hours fasting. As time goes on, after a few weeks when your body gets used to intermittent fasting and new diet plans than switch to longer fasting hours slowly.

According to studies women starting intermittent fasting from 12-16 hours might face a worse level of blood sugar and they might feel tired dizzy and face some other problems including irregular periods and conceiving problems.

Pregnant women or breastfeeding mothers should not start intermittent fasting until and unless they have discussed it with any health expert or doctor. The following are some shorter fasting methods for women. Let's have a look at them.

The fast diet Method:

The fast diet method is also known as the 5:2 diet method. It is an easy intermittent fasting method to start with. It means you have to fast for two days a week and for the rest of 5 weeks take the normal diet. For women, I would recommend not to choose consecutive days of the week. Instead, you can select Monday or Thursday.

Alternative day fasting:

Alternative day fasting is a good method for women, as it allows to eat 25% of total calorie intake while you are fasting. It means women can consume 500 calories during fasting days. Alternative fasting means you have to fast alternate days and can eat normally for the rest of the days.

Crescendo Method:

Crescendo method is also good for women as it allows fasting for only three days of the week. The rest of the take's women should keep taking in their regular meals to maintain body energy. Just make sure not to select the consecutive days.

Whichever method you are going to pick, it is very important to eat well during the non-fasting periods. On the off chance that you eat a lot of unfortunates, calorie enriched fast-food including burgers, fries, oily foods, and sugary beverages during the non-fasting periods, you may not encounter a similar weight reduction and medical advantages.

Toward the day's end, the best methodology is one that you can endure and continue for a long period. Until and unless it is not leaving any negative effect on your body. Keep practicing the method that is best to fulfill all your health desires.

Many people including both men and women just start of intermittent fasting by skipping important meals like breakfast and dinner and assume that they are fasting for good. Skipping meals with your convenience would not give you the desired benefits anytime soon. That is why it is suggested to select any of the above methods and get stick to it. At the end of the day, the most important thing is to follow the methods that suit best to your health and helps you in weight reduction.

Modified versions of intermittent fasting are safe for women. If any women are facing any problem as mentioned follows, they are requested to stop fasting at the very moment and consult your doctor.

· Severe mood swings.

- Fatigue.
- Severe nausea.
- Gasses troubles.
- Tiredness and laziness.
- Hair loss.
- Missed periods.
- Problems in conceiving.
- Constipation.
- Bad breath.
- Low or reduced energy.
- Lack of concentration.

Difference between Fasting and Starving:

Many people confuse fasting with starving. People associate different meanings to different words according to their understanding. Suppose it is a misconception regarding the healthy body. People thinking to starve to death and reducing your weight to the extent that you start looking like a human skeleton means having a healthy body. Well, this point of view is not true at all. Being healthy does not mean to starve and to avoid all the favorite dishes of yours. Healthy eating does not mean that you have to quit every diet plan that was once a favorite of yours. Instead of being healthy means being able to perform your life duties actively and efficiently.

If your body is capable of doing all the life tasks without getting lazy or tired. If you sleep as quickly as you lay down on your bed if your stomach is as powerful to digest all kinds of calories with heartburn and acid reflux if your bones and back do not hurt you. It means that you have a healthy body.

Reducing a lot of pounds from your body does not mean that you have had adopted a healthy lifestyle. A healthy lifestyle is not only limited to reducing weight. It involves numerous other things as well. Same as above people confuse with starving as well. But in fact, there is a huge difference between the two of them. Let's find out how starving and fasting are two different things.

There is a tremendous contrast between fasting and starving. While you are fasting, and eating no calories and food the body will deliberately rinse itself of everything aside from all the extra calories that need to get burn out. Otherwise, they would be harmful to the body. These extra calories are also named as "bad body fats". Fasting is done for a limited period and it is done for all the good reasons. Starvation will happen just when the body is compelled to utilize indispensable tissue to endure.

People adjust incredibly well to the absence of nourishment. A. J. Carlson, Professor of Physiology, University of Chicago, expresses that a solid, all-around fed man can live from 50 to 75 days without nourishment, or without any intake of food, proteins or any other supplements. If he isn't presented to brutal components or enthusiastic pressure. There are various instances of water fasts over the 75-day mark. In all actuality, 75-day water fasts are uncommon, however, it demonstrates that God has brilliantly made the body to have the option to live for expanded periods without nourishment. During the times of wars or natural calamity, people have seen fasting for more than a few months. The only thing that keeps their body going is fluid and water. In some parts of Africa people even start eating tree leaves for their survival.

Human fat is esteemed at 3,500 calories for each pound. Every additional pound of fat will supply enough calories for one day of hard physical work. Ten pounds of fat is equivalent to 35,000 calories! This is proportional to 35 pounds of fish or 192 pounds of carrots, a great incentive for your fat. It indicates that our bodies must be storing a lot of calories that helps to give the body a survival strength during fasting and starving hours.

Every single living thing can endure unforgiving conditions. Life forms can store supplements in the fat, blood, bone marrow and different tissues. Camels are equipped for putting away fat and water in their protuberances; tadpoles go without eating when their legs are creating, subsisting on their tails, which are never again required. The Mexican Gila Monster puts away holds in its tail when nourishment is copious and can make due for about a month and a half when nourishment is rare. The marine iguana of the Galapagos Islands is named the Vegetarian Dragon since it lives on ocean growth. It can go without nourishment for more than one hundred days.

On the other hand, the western world is blessed to have plenty of food and other energy building supplements. Except if engaged with energetic exercise or starvation we do not have the chance to go through the unnecessary fat stores helpfully saved around the growing waistline. That is why people living in western countries need some effective methods to shed those extra pounds and calories that are coming out of their belly and waistline. And no doubt intermittent fasting is one of the effective methods that helps them to shed these extra calories and to continue with life healthily.

Our body goes into a condition of fasting while we rest. With extraordinary persistence, it holds up until we begin resting off, lastly, in the rest state, it starts its supernatural work of purifying. As we have discussed earlier. Breakfast is the most nourishing meal of the day, that is why it is suggested to break your fast at that time and properly nourish your body. After arousing from this short fast, the tongue is covered, breath foul, skin puffy, and the psyche foggy. These are for the most part early side effects of the body in a condition of detoxification, short little occasions have taken each night from the existence of devouring. Bacon, eggs, a side request of flapjacks, and some espresso is a certain method for stopping detoxification obviously, you feel in a split second better, crediting it to an oily breakfast. One of the favors you will encounter later in a fast is bubbly vitality when emerging from the bed toward the beginning of the day. No drowsy soil or puffy eyes; your hair in the flawless spot. A breath is sweet as the morning fog that streams over slopes shrouded in spring blossoms. Fasting, trailed by a solid eating routine, is the method for achieving the introduction of another life.

Though starving and fasting are two different things. But for your convenience, I can explain these terms more easily. In the third world, because of the unavailability of required food people starve to death. The unavailability of necessities of life leads them towards suicides and natural deaths. People aim for one complete meal in a week. But on the other hand, the developed countries, the rich western world waste a lot of food, they fast to throw away extra body calories. Starving is no choice; people have to do it because they do not have food. But fasting is a people's choice, they do it as a fashion or to get rid of extra stored calories.

Summary: A Complete Guide to Fasting

- Intermittent is one of the modified versions of fasting hat has many health-related benefits.

- Intermittent fasting means irregular fasting for several hours that helps the body in the burning of extra stored calories and fats.

- Intermittent fasting is different than starving and other diet methods including keto.

- If not followed properly or without a doctor's suggestion, intermittent fasting might lead you toward health hazards.

- In case of any emergency, it is advised to stop intermittent fasting and get medical care.

- Read safety tips carefully before starting intermittent fasting.
- Intermittent fasting has several methods like 5:2 diet plan, the warrior method, eat stop eat method, 16/8 method, and alternate-day fasting method.
- Pregnant women or breastfeeding women should not go for intermittent fasting without concern with the gynecologist.
- This is the most effective method of weight loss and belly fats reduction.
- Intermittent fasting has different impact on women as compared to men. It might affect women adversely sometimes.
- There are a lot of myths associated with intermittent fasting and all of them are not true. People assume different myths with fasting and its effect. It is suggested to do a better research before jumping to a conclusion.

- No matter what, if you are planning to start intermittent fasting a consultation with a health expert is a must.

That is all. Finally, if you found this book useful in any way, a review on Amazon is always appreciated!